MOVE FIRST

MOVE FIRST

Why Your Brain Will Never Feel Ready

By:

Samantha Teeboon

DEDICATION

For Thomas.
You saved my life before you even knew you could.

And for Jose.
You showed me what love looks like when it doesn't hurt.

And for every abandoned child who became an abandoned adult:
You are worthy. You always have been.

AUTHOR'S NOTE

This book contains descriptions of childhood trauma, abuse, addiction, and suicidal ideation. These are not easy topics to read about, and they weren't easy to write about either. But I believe that honesty—even when it's painful—is the only path to genuine healing.

If you are currently struggling with any of these issues, please know that help is available. You don't have to face this alone. You never did.

National Suicide Prevention Lifeline: 988
National Domestic Violence Hotline: 1-800-799-7233
SAMHSA National Helpline: 1-800-662-4357

Throughout this book, I share both my personal story and insights from psychology, trauma research, and behavioral science. I'm not a therapist—I'm a behavior specialist pursuing my master's in social work. The information in this book is not a substitute for professional mental health treatment. But I hope it offers you something just as valuable: the knowledge that someone else has walked this road and survived it.

Your story matters. Your pain matters. And your healing? That matters most of all.

With love and hope,
Samantha

CONTENTS

INTRODUCTION
Why I Wrote This Book

I was abandoned at four years old.

Left in a dark house for days while my mother disappeared into her addiction. My father came for me. He got me out. But trauma doesn't work that way—being saved from a moment doesn't save you from what it left behind.

I was pregnant at fifteen. Trapped in an abusive relationship at sixteen. A mother escaping with my baby at seventeen.

I spent years drowning—in alcohol, in trauma, in the belief that I was fundamentally broken. Unworthy of love. Unworthy of happiness. Unworthy of the life I secretly dreamed about but never believed I could have.

There were nights I wanted to die. Nights I tried to make that happen.

But I'm still here.

At thirty-five years old, I'm in graduate school studying to become a social worker. I'm married to a man who showed me what love looks like when it doesn't hurt. We raised a son who is breaking every cycle I thought was unbreakable.

How did I get from there to here? That's what this book is about.

But I need to be clear about something from the start: this book is not about having it all figured out. I don't. This book is about the messy, painful, beautiful process of learning to believe you're worthy—even when everything in your life has told you otherwise.

I wrote this book because I needed it. When I was at my lowest—drunk, suicidal, convinced I was beyond saving—I needed someone to tell me that transformation was possible. Not in a motivational-poster kind of way, but in a real, honest, here's-what-it-actually-looks-like kind of way.

I needed someone who'd been where I was to tell me the truth: that healing isn't pretty, that recovery isn't linear, that some days you'll feel like you're right back where you started. But also that it's worth it. That you can build a life you never thought possible. That the darkness doesn't have to be the end of your story.

I couldn't find that book. So I wrote it.

How This Book Works

Each chapter follows a simple structure: my story, the science behind it, and reflection questions for your own journey. The reflections aren't homework—they're invitations. Skip them or sit with them. This is your journey.

I want to be honest with you about something else, too: my story includes difficult content. Abandonment. Abuse. Addiction. Suicidal ideation. I don't share these things for shock value or sympathy. I share them because they're true, and because I believe that honesty is the only path to real connection.

If you're reading this from your darkest moment—I see you. I've been there. And I need you to know: it can get better. Not quickly. Not easily. But it can.

You are worthy. You always have been.

Let me show you how I finally learned to believe it.

WHAT THIS BOOK WILL TEACH YOU

This book is three things:

1. A memoir—the raw, unpolished truth of what I lived through.
2. A science book—not a textbook, but a translation of what researchers have discovered about how change actually works.
3. A practical guide—tools, exercises, and questions to help you apply what you learn.

Throughout, you'll meet some of the most important psychologists of the last century: William James, who showed that action creates emotion. Martin Seligman, who discovered learned helplessness—and how to unlearn it. Viktor Frankl, who found meaning in concentration camps. Angela Duckworth, who proved that grit beats talent. Carol Dweck, whose growth mindset research shows our beliefs shape what we become. BJ Fogg, who revolutionized behavior change with tiny habits. Kelly McGonigal, who discovered that our beliefs about stress matter more than the stress itself. Kristin Neff, who proved that self-compassion is a strength. Albert Bandura, who showed that self-belief is built through doing.

You don't need to become a psychology expert. I'll explain everything in plain language. By the end, you'll understand not just what to do—but why it works.

THE FRAMEWORK

When I talk about kids throwing chairs, I'm not really talking about kids. I'm talking about nervous systems. And you have one too.

The adult version of throwing a chair is opening Instagram instead of the blank document. It's saying "I'll start Monday" for the forty-seventh time. It's having fourteen half-finished projects. It's knowing exactly what to do and still feeling unable to make yourself do it. Same biology. Same protection. Different behavior.

This shows up everywhere — when you're trying to change your career, your health, your relationships, your finances, or finally start the thing you've been thinking about for years.

We don't outgrow the parts of us that freeze, avoid, control, or shut down. We just learn more socially acceptable ways to act them out.

You don't need a dramatic past to recognize yourself here. A nervous system doesn't need catastrophe to learn protection — it only needs experience.

This is why what actually creates change in children is the same thing that creates change in adults. Not pressure. Not discipline. Not better plans.

Safety comes first. For adults, safety is what you create when you stop attacking yourself for being stuck. When you notice you're scrolling and instead of "What is wrong with me?" you say, "Something in me doesn't feel safe yet." When you regulate before you strategize. When you change the environment before you change the goal. Sometimes safety looks like closing ten tabs instead of opening a new planner. Sometimes it's taking a walk before making a life decision. Sometimes it's eating, sleeping, breathing, and lowering the volume on your world.

Once safety is there, agency becomes possible. Not massive goals. Not identity overhauls. Small, chosen actions. The adult version of "do you want to sit here or there?" is "Do I want to open the document or write one sentence?" "Do I want to draft the email or just title it?" "Do I want to put my shoes on or step outside?" Agency is what tells your nervous system, *I still choose. I'm not being forced.* And that's what keeps it from snapping back into defense.

Capacity is what grows next. Capacity is your ability to stay with discomfort without escaping. To start and not immediately quit. To be seen without vanishing. To do something imperfectly and not use it as proof that you should stop. Every time you resist the urge to avoid, every time you touch the edge of something new and come back safe, your nervous system updates. You can tolerate more. You can hold more. You can try again. Capacity is not talent. It's tolerance.

And this is the order that actually creates change: safety first, agency second, capacity third, growth last. If you skip the first three, growth will always feel like force. But when you build them in this order, something quiet and powerful happens.

You stop trying to become someone else. And you start becoming someone who can move.

That's what this book is really about. That's what fifteen years of working with struggling kids taught me. And that's the framework everything else hangs on.

How to Read This Book

Go slow. Do the reflection questions at the end of each chapter—not as homework, but as invitations to apply what you're learning. Write in the margins. Take breaks when you need to.

Most importantly: don't just read. Do.

"Move First" is the framework this book is built on: action precedes feeling. Each chapter applies this principle to a different challenge. Throughout, you'll see the phrase "Move first. The feeling catches up" as a reminder to keep going—even when you don't feel ready.

So let's begin.

Before you turn another page — scan this.

Get your free guide: *5 Questions to Ask Before You Leap*

Samanthateeboon.com/free-guide

CHAPTER 1
THE WOUND
Move First... Even When Your Past Says You're Broken

Part 1: My Story

I don't remember all of it. I was four, and memory at that age is more feeling than fact. But I remember enough.

I remember being hungry. Not the kind of hungry that comes before dinner, but the kind that makes your stomach ache and your head feel hollow. I remember the house being dark—curtains closed, lights off, or maybe there were no lights at all. Day or night, I couldn't tell. At four, time doesn't work right. Time is just waiting.

I don't remember my mother being there. She wasn't. That's the point.

What I remember instead is silence. The heavy, too-much silence of a house where a child is alone. My older siblings were supposed to watch me—that's what someone told me later. But they were kids themselves, and kids can't parent. They must have left at some point. Or maybe they were never really there.

I don't remember how many days I was alone. Someone told me later it was three. Someone else said five. Does it matter? To a four-year-old, one day alone feels like forever.

What I remember clearly is the door opening. Light flooding in. A shape in the doorway. A man's voice—rough with something I didn't yet have a name for. Anger, maybe. Fear. Or both.

"Sam!"

That was my father. That was the moment he found me.

The neighbors had called him. They'd noticed things—a child who should have been outside playing but wasn't, curtains that never opened, no sign of my mother for days. In the 90s, people still looked out for each other's kids, at least sometimes. Someone made a phone call. My father came.

He picked me up—I remember that part. The feeling of being lifted, of arms around me, solid and real. He smelled like work, like outside, like something that wasn't this house. He held me tight against his chest, and I remember the strange sensation of being held after days of not being touched at all.

"We're going home," he said into my hair. "You're coming with me."

Home. I didn't know what that meant anymore.

I'd been living with my mother since my parents split— though "living" might be too generous a word for what we were doing. I had been existing in that house, cared for by no one, babysat by silence and hunger and the endless waiting for someone to remember I was there.

That day, home meant my father's house. Home meant leaving.

He carried me out to his car. I don't remember the neighbors watching, but they must have been. They must have stood at their windows with the particular ache adults feel when they witness a child's life going wrong in real time.

What I know now—what I didn't know then—is that being rescued isn't the same as being safe. Leaving one kind of trauma often means walking straight into another.

My father came for me when I needed him most. He was fighting his own battles—addiction, exhaustion, a life that had never taught him how to heal, let alone how to help a child heal. He loved me. He just didn't have the tools.

I never doubted that he loved me. But love doesn't automatically know how to care for a traumatized child. He was fighting his own battles. I was fighting mine. We didn't know how to fight them together.

Still—on that day, in that moment, when the door opened and light poured in—I was saved.

It would take decades to understand that being saved once doesn't protect you from needing to be saved again and again. That rescue is only the beginning, not the end. That the wound opened in that dark house would shape everything that came after—my relationships, my choices, my struggles, my entire life.

That was my first wound.

The one that taught me I was forgettable.

Leave-able.

Not quite worth staying for.

It wasn't my last.

Nights at the Bar

The nights at the bar were restless.

I'd sit on a barstool too tall for my small body, my feet dangling above the sticky floor, watching my father drink while the hours crawled by. The air was thick with cigarette smoke and spilled beer—smells that still pull me backward in time whenever I encounter them, even now.

To keep myself occupied, I played games on the TV screens mounted along the bar—the kind meant for adults, not children. I learned quickly which games were safe. Solitaire was safe. Trivia was safe. Anything else risked an image flashing across the screen that a five-year-old shouldn't see. I became skilled at clicking away before my eyes could register what was there.

A child shouldn't have to learn that skill. A child shouldn't know what to avoid on an adults-only screen. But that was my normal.

The bartender became my friend—or what passed for a friend when you're a kid in a bar. She looked out for me in her own quiet way, bringing chicken fingers, fries, and mozzarella sticks without being asked. I think she felt sorry for me, this little girl perched on a barstool night after night while her father drank himself into oblivion. Food was her way of taking care of me when nobody else could.

Sometimes, when the bar was slow—those dead weeknights when only the serious drinkers showed up—I'd wander over to the pool table. It felt like an adventure, leaving my post to explore this grown-up world I'd been dropped into. I'd roll the balls around, pretend I knew how to play, invent games to pass the time.

Looking back now, I understand why I was only allowed near the pool table when it was quiet. On busy nights, that back corner was where people did drugs. I know that now, with adult eyes. They kept me away from it, at least. Small mercies.

From my barstool, I watched everything. I studied the regulars, learned their patterns, figured out who was safe and who wasn't. I watched the bartender cut people off. I watched fights start. I watched people stumble out into the night.

I was learning lessons no child should have to learn. How to read a room for danger. How to disappear when the energy shifted. How to entertain myself for hours with nothing but a screen and a basket of fries. How to survive in places that were never meant for me.

Those nights shaped me in ways I'm still uncovering. They taught me hypervigilance—always scanning, always alert. They taught me self-reliance—if I needed something, I had to figure it out myself. They taught me that adults weren't always reliable, that love and presence weren't the same thing, that being physically there didn't mean being emotionally available.

My father loved me. I never doubted that.
But love didn't stop him from placing me on that barstool night after night.
It didn't stop addiction from coming first.
It didn't protect me from an environment no child should know.

He loved me—and he couldn't protect me.
Both things were true.

What I Learned

Childhood doesn't teach you lessons in neat sentences. It teaches you through repetition. Through silence. Through what never happens.

I didn't sit down one day and decide who I would become.

My nervous system decided for me.

I learned not to ask.

Not because I didn't need things, but because asking didn't change anything. Asking made adults sigh. Asking made them annoyed. Asking made me visible in ways that didn't feel safe. So I learned to swallow my needs before they ever reached my mouth.

I learned to wait.

I learned how to wait quietly, patiently, without expectation. I learned how to sit with hunger. With boredom. With uncertainty. I learned how to wait for rides, for food, for attention, for something to change. Waiting became my default state. Movement felt risky. Stillness felt safer.

I learned to read adults instead of trusting them.

I learned to watch faces, tones, body language. I learned to tell who was sober enough to talk to, who was angry enough to avoid, who might explode, and who might ignore me entirely. I became fluent in moods before I was fluent in my own feelings. Trust wasn't something you gave—it was something you calculated.

I learned that love could exist without protection.

This one took the longest to understand. My father loved me. I never doubted that. But love didn't stop him from leaving me alone in adult spaces. It didn't stop addiction from running the show. It didn't stop harm. I learned that love, on its own, didn't mean safety. And once you learn that, it's hard to unlearn.

I learned that needing less made me safer.

The less I asked for, the less disappointed I was. The less I needed, the less there was to take away. I learned how to shrink my wants until they barely registered. I learned how to convince myself I was fine, even when I wasn't. Especially when I wasn't.

None of these lessons were taught out loud. They were absorbed. And they didn't feel like damage at the time. They felt like intelligence. Like adaptation. Like maturity beyond my years.

They kept me functioning. They kept me alive.

But they also followed me into adulthood.

The waiting turned into procrastination and paralysis. The silence turned into difficulty asking for help. The hyper-awareness turned into anxiety. The belief that love doesn't protect turned into choosing unsafe relationships. The habit of needing less turned into chronic self-abandonment.

For a long time, I thought these were just personality traits. I thought this was simply who I was. I didn't realize they were survival strategies. I didn't realize they were learned. And I didn't realize that what's learned can be unlearned.

Part 2: Understanding the Wound

I don't tell you this story because my trauma is special—it isn't. Trauma is devastatingly common. According to the CDC, about 61% of adults have experienced at least one Adverse Childhood Experience, and nearly one in six has experienced four or more.

I tell you my story because for decades, I didn't understand what had happened to me. I thought I was broken. Damaged. Different in some fundamental, unfixable way.

I didn't know what I experienced had a name. I didn't know that abandonment at four literally rewires a developing brain. I didn't know that the fear, emptiness, and desperate need to be seen that followed me into adulthood weren't flaws—they were wounds.

Understanding trauma changed everything. Not because it erased the past, but because it gave me a framework. When you understand *why* you do what you do, you finally gain the power to change it.

What Is Trauma, Really?

Trauma isn't about what happened to you. It's about how your nervous system responded to what happened.

Trauma occurs when an experience overwhelms our ability to cope. Two people can go through the same event, and one may be traumatized while the other isn't. That doesn't mean one is stronger or weaker. It means their nervous systems processed the experience differently.

For a four-year-old left alone for days, everything is overwhelming. There's no cognitive ability to understand why a parent hasn't returned. No emotional regulation to self-soothe. No life experience to know this will end.

There is only terror. Abandonment. And the growing certainty of being forgotten.

A child's brain encodes that experience in ways meant to ensure survival—and those adaptations can follow us for decades.

Complex PTSD: When Trauma Repeats

Learning about Complex PTSD gave me language for my life.

C-PTSD differs from single-incident trauma because it results from prolonged, repeated exposure—especially during childhood and especially when caregivers are involved.

The abandonment at four was only the beginning. What followed—the addiction, instability, neglect, and later abuse—layered trauma upon trauma until I couldn't tell where one wound ended and another began.

C-PTSD doesn't just create flashbacks or nightmares. It shapes identity. It alters how you relate to others, how you regulate emotion, how you see yourself. It creates survival strategies that look like personality traits—hypervigilance, people-pleasing, emotional numbing, difficulty trusting.

For most of my life, I thought I was just "too much" or "not enough." It never occurred to me that these weren't character flaws. They were adaptations.

Honoring Your Pain:

For years, I minimized what happened to me.
Other people had it worse.
At least someone came for me.
At least I survived.

This is what trauma survivors do. We compare. We downplay. We convince ourselves our pain doesn't count.

But pain isn't a competition.

Your wound doesn't have to be the worst to matter. It just has to be yours.

Honoring your pain means telling the truth. Not to wallow. Not to blame. But to heal. You can't heal what you refuse to acknowledge.

Reflection: Naming Your Wound

Take a moment—no writing required.

What was your first wound?

How old were you?

What did it teach you about yourself, about others, about the world?

This is for you. The beginning of seeing your story clearly.

You can't heal what you won't acknowledge.

And now, you've begun.

CHAPTER 2
WORTH
Move First… Even When You Don't Feel Deserving

Part 1: My Story

After my father rescued me, I went to live with him. People often assume that's where the story turns hopeful. In some ways, it did. I was no longer alone in a dark house, waiting to be remembered. But safety isn't just about being found. It's about being protected. And that part never quite arrived.

My father loved me. I never doubted that. But he was an alcoholic, and alcoholism fractures love. It makes care inconsistent. Sometimes affection is overwhelming. Other times it disappears entirely. For a child, that inconsistency becomes its own form of danger—because you never know which version of love you're going to get.

By the time I was five or six, I spent most nights in bars with him. He'd place me on a barstool, order me a Shirley Temple, and drink while I waited. Sometimes I fell asleep right there, curled against the wood, surrounded by conversations that weren't meant for children. I didn't know this wasn't normal. I didn't know other kids weren't learning how to entertain themselves for hours in smoky rooms while their parent got drunk. I just knew this was my life, and like children do, I adapted to it without question.

I became good at reading moods. I learned when it was safe to speak and when it wasn't. I learned how to make myself small, how to disappear without actually leaving. These skills helped me survive, but they also quietly shaped how I saw myself. I didn't yet have words for it, but I was learning that my needs were inconvenient and my presence was something to manage carefully.

It was at the bar that my dad and I met, let's call her Dar.

She was a woman my father knew—a regular, someone in his orbit. She had a daughter around my age named Nikki. For a while, Dar and my father "dated," and Nikki and I became something like friends. Sometimes we played together. Sometimes Dar took me to her house for sleepovers.

Nikki had a best friend named Danielle. She was around our age, someone who was often with us, someone familiar enough to feel part of the background of those days. I don't remember details about what she looked like, and I don't trust myself to invent them now. What I remember isn't her appearance, it's her presence. She was there. Close enough that what happened next would stay with me forever.

One night, I slept over at Dar's house. My father was meant to pick me up the next day. But the next day came, and he didn't show. Hours passed. Dar needed to go somewhere—to a car derby of some kind—and she couldn't wait any longer. So she loaded all three of us into the car: me, Nikki, and Danielle.

I don't remember the drive. Trauma does that—it erases the before and leaves only the during.

What I remember is the crash.

The sound.

The impact.

The way the world spun and then stopped.

And then Danielle.

She was in my lap. She was bleeding. Her small body was broken in ways I didn't understand and couldn't process. She died in my arms. I was six years old, and a child died in my arms.

I don't remember everything after that. I remember the hospital. I remember stitches—I still carry the scars on my face. I remember my dad coming to get me, probably overwhelmed in his own way. And then I remember being home. Just home. Like nothing had happened.

No one talked to me about it. No one asked if I was okay. There was no counseling, no explanation, no space to grieve. I didn't attend a funeral. I didn't say goodbye. The message was unspoken but unmistakable: this was something to survive, not something to process.

So I did what children do when they aren't helped to make sense of pain. I buried it. I put it wherever kids put the things that are too big to hold. And I moved on into the next chapter of a childhood that kept reinforcing the same lesson in different forms.

Your pain doesn't count.

You're lucky to be alive.

Don't complain.

Other people had it worse.

I believed that for a very long time.

What I didn't realize then was that this was where my sense of worth began to fracture. Not because trauma happened, but because it went unacknowledged. When no one responds to your pain, you start to believe it doesn't matter. And when your pain doesn't matter, it doesn't take long to conclude that you don't either.

Worth isn't something children decide. It's something they absorb from how adults respond to their needs. And what I absorbed, over and over, was that my pain was survivable— but not significant.

That belief followed me everywhere.

The Little Teacher (Why This Matters)
Even while I was learning that my pain didn't matter, something else was happening quietly inside me. I wanted to be a teacher.

Teachers were the most consistent adults in my life. They showed up. They followed routines. They noticed when someone was struggling. They created order where my life had very little. At home, I lined up my stuffed animals and dolls and taught them. I stood at an imaginary chalkboard, giving lessons to an invisible classroom. In those moments, I wasn't a burden or an inconvenience. I was capable. I was important.

But I didn't have supplies. No chalk. No worksheets. No stickers. So I started taking them. At first it was small—a pencil, an eraser. Over time it escalated. By second grade, I was bringing home backpacks full of supplies: markers, crayons, paper, even teacher manuals. Everything I needed to run my classroom.

I didn't think of it as stealing. I thought of it as necessity. Teachers needed supplies. I wanted to be one.

When I was caught, I was forced to return everything. I remember the shame of walking back into that school, handing over the supplies, apologizing to adults whose approval mattered deeply to me. It was humiliating. But what stays with me now is not the embarrassment—it's what didn't happen. No one asked why. No one wondered what a child was trying to build. No one connected the behavior to unmet needs or a chaotic home.

I wasn't a bad kid. I was a child trying to create safety and control in the only way I knew how. Even then, without language for it, I was trying to move first.

Part 2: Understanding Worth and Shame

For years, I believed these experiences meant something about me—that I was fundamentally unworthy. That belief didn't come from one dramatic moment. It came from repetition. From silence. From being expected to endure without acknowledgment. This is where shame is born.

Guilt says, "I did something bad." Shame says, "I am bad." Guilt focuses on behavior. Shame attacks identity. When children experience trauma that goes ignored or minimized, they don't have the cognitive capacity to blame circumstance or adult failure. Instead, they personalize it. If no one protected me, I must not be worth protecting. If no one asked how I felt, my feelings must not matter.

Surviving the accident added another layer. Why did Danielle die and not me? My child brain didn't land on chance. It landed on meaning. There's nothing special about you. You just got lucky. Don't waste it. Don't complain. That belief shaped how I treated myself for decades.

This is how worth becomes conditional. I'm worthy if I'm easy. I'm worthy if I don't need much. I'm worthy if I survive quietly.

Inherent worth means you matter because you exist. Conditional worth means you matter if you meet requirements. Trauma teaches conditional worth. It teaches us to earn space instead of occupy it, to survive instead of live. Unlearning that takes time, repetition, and action.

Part 3: Reclaiming Worth Through Action

Here's what both research and lived experience confirm: you don't build worth by thinking differently. You build it by doing differently. Confidence and self-belief emerge through mastery experiences—through showing up, trying, failing, and trying again.

Every time you act despite feeling undeserving, you gather evidence that challenges the old story. That's why Move First matters. You don't wait to feel worthy. You act, and worth follows.

Reflection: Rewriting Your Worth Story

What did your childhood teach you about worth?

What did you learn you had to do—or not do—to be accepted?

Where are you still living by those old rules?

You don't need answers yet. Just awareness. Because once you see the pattern, you can begin to interrupt it.

Move first. Even when you don't feel deserving.
Your worth will catch up.

CHAPTER 3
HARDSHIP
Move First... Even When Everyone Expects You to Fail

Part 1: My Story

By the time I was twelve, I had perfected the art of leaving without being noticed.

I didn't climb out windows or sneak off dramatically. I left through the door, the same door everyone else used. I just knew how to do it quietly. I knew which spots on the stairs creaked and which ones didn't. I knew how to turn the handle slowly so it wouldn't click, how to ease the door open without the hinge groaning, how to step outside without announcing myself to the house. These weren't skills I learned because I was adventurous or thrill-seeking. I learned them because I was paying attention. Because when a home doesn't feel safe or steady, you learn how to move through it without leaving a trace.

Leaving felt easier than staying.

Home wasn't abusive in obvious ways, but it wasn't grounding either. It was unpredictable, emotionally inconsistent, and heavy with things that were never said out loud. Silence can be just as unsettling as chaos. So I learned how to slip away quietly, how to disappear without causing a reaction, how to exit without drawing attention. That ability to move unnoticed would follow me for years, long after sneaking out stopped being literal and started becoming emotional.

I wasn't alone. I had a whole crew of friends who were doing the same thing—kids from school whose home lives were just as chaotic as mine, who were running from the same kinds of pain even if the specifics were different. We found each other the way damaged kids always do, drawn together by some invisible magnetism of shared struggle.

It was the early 2000s, and rebellion felt like a rite of passage. Looking back now, with the perspective of someone who works with traumatized kids, I can see what we were really doing. We weren't just being "bad kids." We were self-medicating. We were escaping. We were screaming for help in the only language we knew.

But back then, it just felt like living.

I skipped school constantly. Not just occasionally—constantly. Whole days, sometimes whole weeks. My friends and I would meet up somewhere, anywhere that wasn't where we were supposed to be, and we'd spend our days doing all the things teenagers aren't supposed to do. Drinking. Smoking. Getting into trouble that felt thrilling in the moment and empty afterward.

Even when I showed up to school, I'd skip individual classes. I knew every hiding spot, every unlocked door, every blind spot in the hallways where teachers didn't patrol. Education felt pointless when you couldn't see a future worth preparing for.

I don't blame my parents—not entirely, anyway. They were doing the best they could with what they had, and what they had wasn't much. My father was battling his own demons. He didn't have the tools to help me because no one had ever given him those tools either.

That's the thing about generational trauma—it's not about blame. It's about patterns that repeat because no one ever learned a different way. My parents' childhoods weren't any better than mine. Their parents' childhoods weren't any better than theirs. The dysfunction just kept flowing downhill, generation after generation, because that's what dysfunction does when no one stops to interrupt it.

So, I ran wild. I tested every limit, pushed every boundary, dared the universe to show me that someone cared enough to stop me.

Nobody did. Or maybe they tried and I was too far gone to notice.

My biological mother had resurfaced by then. After years of absence—jail, addiction, choosing drugs over me—she suddenly wanted to be part of my life again. I was around eight when she came back, and I remember feeling... nothing. Not relief, not anger, not joy. Just a hollow emptiness where a mother-daughter bond should have been.

There was no connection. How could there be? You can't abandon a child for years and then expect to pick up where you left off as if nothing happened. The damage was done. The attachment that should have formed in those early years—the secure base that children need to feel safe in the world—never developed. She was a stranger who happened to share my DNA.

But I used her. I'm not proud of this, but it's the truth. Between ages twelve and sixteen, I bounced between my parents' houses like a pinball, going wherever it suited me in the moment. My mother's house meant freedom—no rules, no supervision, no one paying attention to what I did. My father's house meant rules, which I resented but also secretly craved.

I played them against each other. Manipulated situations to get what I wanted. Took advantage of their guilt and their dysfunction and their inability to communicate with each other.

I was a survivor, doing whatever it took to navigate an impossible situation. But I was also a wounded kid making choices that would have consequences I couldn't yet imagine.

And then I met P.

The Trap

It started the way these things always start: normal.

We hung out. We drank together. We had fun—or what passed for fun when you're a teenager with no supervision and too much freedom. He was older, which felt exciting. He paid attention to me, which felt intoxicating. After years of feeling invisible, of feeling like I didn't matter, here was someone who seemed to see me.

I didn't know then what I know now: that predators are skilled at identifying vulnerable targets. That the attention I was so desperate for was actually a trap being set. That by the time I realized what was happening, I would already be caught.

The signs were there from the beginning, if I'd known how to read them. He was cheating on me within the first few months—I found out later it had been going on the whole time. One of the girls was supposed to be my best friend. The betrayal cut deep, but I was already in too far to walk away. Or at least, that's what I told myself.

Then I got pregnant.

I was fifteen years old, and I was going to be a mother. The news hit me like a physical blow—terror and disbelief and a strange, fierce protectiveness that surprised me with its intensity. Whatever else was true, whatever mess I'd made of my life, there was now a life inside me that I was responsible for.

That's when everything changed.

The abuse didn't start with a punch. It never does. It started with my clothes.

"You're not wearing that." Said casually at first, like a suggestion. Then more firmly. Then as a command that wasn't open for discussion. My wardrobe shrank as his control expanded—nothing too tight, nothing too short, nothing that might attract attention from other men. I told myself it was because he loved me, because he was protective, because he cared.

Then came the friends.

One by one, he cut them off. This one was a bad influence. That one was trying to break us up. The other one couldn't be trusted. He had a reason for each one, and the reasons sounded almost logical if you didn't look too closely. Before I knew it, I had no one left. The crew I used to sneak out with, the girls I used to skip school with—they were all gone. Pushed away or driven away or simply forbidden.

Then came my family.

The isolation was systematic and complete. He didn't just want me to stop seeing them—he wanted to erase any evidence they'd ever existed. I wasn't allowed to keep anything that reminded me of my life before him. Pictures disappeared. Mementos were thrown away. Childhood photos, school photos, pictures of friends—all of it, gone. It was like he was trying to erase my entire history, to make me believe that my life only started when I met him.

Any time I showed emotion about what I'd lost—any time I mentioned missing someone or wanting to see my family—it started a fight. And fights with P were terrifying. So I learned to suppress it all. I pushed down the grief, the loneliness, the desperate longing for connection. I made myself small and quiet and agreeable, because that was the only way to survive.

By the time we got our own place, I was completely isolated. And that's when the real imprisonment began.

The Window

Our apartment was above a restaurant where P worked. It was small and cramped and became my entire world, because I literally wasn't allowed to leave.

Not to go to the store. Not to take a walk. Not to visit anyone or do anything or exist anywhere outside those walls. I was sixteen years old, pregnant, and trapped in a cage disguised as a home.

P went to work every day in the restaurant downstairs. I could hear him sometimes—his voice carrying up through the floor, laughing with coworkers, living a life that included other people. Meanwhile, I sat alone in our apartment, watching the hours crawl by, waiting for him to come home and hoping he'd be in a good mood.

Here's the part that still breaks my heart when I think about it:

Our apartment faced the place where my father worked.

Every morning, I would stand at the window and watch him. My dad—the man who had rescued me from that dark house when I was four, who loved me even though he didn't know how to show it, who had no idea his daughter was being held prisoner just across the way.

I watched him arrive for work. I watched him load his work truck. I watched him leave to install appliances in customer homes. And he never knew I was there. He never looked up. He never saw me standing at that window, desperate and alone and so close and yet completely unreachable.

I couldn't call out to him. I couldn't wave. I couldn't do anything that might alert P to the fact that I was watching, that I was longing for rescue, that I hadn't completely surrendered to my captivity.

So I just watched. Silent. Invisible. A ghost haunting her own life.

We never had enough food. We struggled constantly to pay bills. I was scared every single day—scared of P's moods, scared of making him angry, scared of what would happen to me and my baby if I did something wrong.

When Thomas was born, I thought maybe things would get better. That P would see him and soften somehow, that "fatherhood" would change him the way motherhood was changing me.

It didn't.

Now I was trapped with a newborn. Still not allowed to leave. Still isolated from everyone who might have helped me. Still performing the exhausting dance of keeping P happy while caring for an infant who needed me constantly.

The apartment stopped heating that winter. We had a baby, and our home was freezing, and we had to move. I thought maybe a new place would mean a new start.

Instead, things got worse.

Finding My Courage

In the new apartment complex, I found something unexpected: a babysitting job.

It wasn't much—just watching a neighbor's kids for a few hours here and there. But it was money I earned myself. It was interaction with other human beings. It was a tiny crack in the walls of my isolation.

And slowly, something started to shift inside me.

Maybe it was the money giving me a sense of independence I hadn't felt in years. Maybe it was seeing how other families functioned, realizing that what I was living wasn't normal. Maybe it was just the natural consequence of time—the fog of abuse starting to thin enough for me to see my situation clearly.

Whatever it was, I started pushing back. Small resistances at first. Tiny assertions of my own will. Nothing dramatic— just the slow, quiet gathering of courage.

The control had become suffocating. Every aspect of my life was dictated by his moods, his rules, his need to dominate every decision I made. I had learned to comply with everything just to keep the peace—because not complying meant conflict, and conflict with P was dangerous.

But something in me was shifting. Maybe it was the babysitting job giving me a taste of independence. Maybe it was watching other families and realizing this wasn't normal.

Maybe I was just tired—bone-deep exhausted from walking on eggshells every single day.

One day, I stood up for myself. I don't even remember what it was about—something small, something that shouldn't have mattered. But I pushed back. I said no.

And he pulled a knife on me.

The police came. Somehow—I don't remember how— the police were called and they showed up at our door. But P was a narcissist, charming and manipulative, and he talked his way out of it. Nothing could be proven, he said. It was a misunderstanding, he said. Look at him, so calm and reasonable, clearly not the kind of person who would threaten his girlfriend with a weapon.

The cops left. I was still trapped. And I knew, with absolute certainty, that I had to get out.

Within weeks, I was gone.

I was seventeen years old. Thomas was seven months old. I had no money, no plan, no clear idea of where I was going or how I was going to survive. All I knew was that I couldn't stay. That staying meant dying—maybe physically, definitely spiritually. That my son deserved a mother who was alive in every sense of the word.

So I left.

Years later—just a few years ago, actually—I learned something that validated everything I'd experienced. P had done the exact same thing to several other women after me. Textbook identical: the isolation, the control, the escalation, the violence. The same pattern, repeated over and over with different victims.

For a long time, I wondered if I had exaggerated what happened to me. If maybe it wasn't as bad as I remembered. If maybe I was being dramatic or unfair or seeing abuse where there was just a difficult relationship.

Learning about the other women erased those doubts. I wasn't exaggerating. I wasn't being dramatic. I was a victim of a predator who had a pattern, and I was lucky—so incredibly lucky—to have gotten out when I did.

Some of those other women weren't as lucky. And I carry them with me, these strangers who share my story, as a reminder of what I escaped and why it matters that I speak the truth about what happened.

The Escape

When people imagine leaving an abusive relationship, they picture something dramatic. Throwing clothes in a bag in the middle of the night. Running out the door while he's not home. A movie moment of escape.

That's not how it happened for me.

My escape was gradual, unfolding over the course of a few days. It started with a phone call to my father—the first real conversation we'd had in a while. I told him I wanted him to meet Thomas, his grandson. Could we come visit?

He said yes.

I don't know if he sensed something in my voice, or if he was just happy to hear from me, or if some part of him knew his daughter was in trouble and this was her way of reaching out. Whatever he understood or didn't understand, he opened the door.

A few days later, I had the conversation I'd been building toward. I told my father I needed to leave my current situation. That I couldn't stay where I was anymore. That Thomas and I needed a place to go.

And he let us move in.

Just like that. No questions, no judgment, no conditions. Whatever complicated history existed between us, whatever disappointments and failures had marked our relationship—in that moment, my father was exactly what I needed him to be. A safe place to land.

Coming back to my childhood home felt like a homecoming and a displacement all at once. The rooms were familiar, but I wasn't the same person who had left them. I was seventeen now, a mother, a survivor of things I couldn't fully name yet. I moved through spaces I'd known my whole life feeling like a stranger, like a guest in my own history.

The awkwardness was thick. The house was different now too. I didn't know how to fit into whatever routine he'd established in my absence. We circled each other awkwardly — a father and daughter, two people who loved each other but didn't quite know how to share space anymore.

And underneath everything was fear...

Fear of *him* showing up angry, making a scene, demanding I come back. Fear of the retaliation that might come for having the audacity to leave.

I spent those first weeks looking over my shoulder, flinching at unexpected sounds, half-expecting every knock at the door to be him. The cage I'd escaped from had been physical, but the fear followed me. It would be a long time before I felt truly safe.

I don't remember much about those early months. Trauma does that—blurs the details, compresses time, leaves only fragments. I remember exhaustion. I remember trying to figure out how to be a mother at seventeen with no resources and no roadmap. I remember feeling simultaneously grateful to be free and terrified of what came next.

And then, about four to six months later, I met Jose.

But that's another chapter.

What Hardship Taught Me

Looking back, I can see how each piece of hardship—the rebellious years, the abusive relationship, the desperate escape—was shaping me into someone stronger than I knew.

The rebellion taught me that I had a survival instinct, even when it expressed itself in destructive ways. The abuse taught me what I would and wouldn't tolerate—eventually. The escape taught me that I was capable of choosing myself and my son, even when every odd was stacked against us.

None of this was inspiration in the moment. It was just survival. Raw, ugly, desperate survival.

But survival is its own kind of triumph. And sometimes, the hardest things we go through become the foundation for everything we build afterward.

When my father found out I was pregnant, he didn't warn me gently or express fear for my future. He said something sharper than that. He told me he had wasted fifteen years on me.

Those words landed harder than any prediction ever could. Not because they were loud, but because they confirmed something I had already begun to believe—that all the effort it took to love me had been for nothing. That whatever hope existed for me had already expired.

I didn't hear concern in his voice. I heard finality. And once a child hears that kind of final judgment, it doesn't inspire change. It teaches resignation.

But probability isn't destiny. And sometimes, the very thing that should destroy you becomes the thing that saves you.

Thomas saved me. Not because a child should have to save their parent—they shouldn't, and the weight of that responsibility isn't fair to put on anyone, let alone a baby. But because his existence gave me something I'd never had before: a reason to fight for a different future.

I will not end up like her.

I will not abandon my child.

I will not let my son grow up the way I did.

That was my first taste of real purpose. Not happiness—that would come much later. Not healing—that was still years away. Just purpose. A reason to keep going when everything in me wanted to give up.

That's what hardship as a catalyst looks like. Not inspiration. Not motivation. Just raw, desperate survival—and the tiny seed of hope that survival might lead to something better.

Part 2: The Science of Growth Through Adversity

Post-Traumatic Growth: When Struggle Leads to Strength

We talk a lot about post-traumatic stress disorder, but far less about its counterpart: post-traumatic growth. Psychologists Richard Tedeschi and Lawrence Calhoun coined this term to describe the positive psychological change that can emerge from the struggle with highly challenging life circumstances.

This doesn't mean trauma is good. It doesn't mean we should seek out suffering or minimize the pain people experience. What it means is that humans have a remarkable capacity to find meaning in suffering—to use our worst experiences as catalysts for becoming who we were meant to be.

Research shows that many trauma survivors report experiencing at least one of five types of growth: greater appreciation for life, improved relationships with others, recognition of new possibilities or paths, increased personal strength, and spiritual or existential change.

For me, the growth came slowly. It wasn't immediate, and it wasn't guaranteed. But looking back, I can see how each hardship—the abandonment, the rebellion, the abuse, the escape—taught me something I couldn't have learned any other way.

Survival taught me I was stronger than I thought. Motherhood taught me I was capable of unconditional love. Escaping abuse taught me I was worth protecting—even if I had to be the one to protect myself.

The Psychology of Abusive Relationships

People often ask abuse survivors: "Why didn't you just leave?" It's a question that reveals a fundamental misunderstanding of how abuse works.

Abuse rarely starts with violence. It starts with love-bombing—overwhelming attention and affection that feels intoxicating, especially to someone who's been starved for love. Then comes the gradual erosion: small criticisms, subtle controls, isolation disguised as protection.

By the time the abuse becomes obvious, the victim is already trapped—financially, emotionally, psychologically. Their support system has been dismantled. Their self-worth has been demolished. They've been conditioned to believe that the abuse is their fault, that they deserve it, that no one else would want them.

Leaving isn't just a decision—it's an act of extraordinary courage that requires overcoming not just external barriers but internal ones. The psychological chains are often stronger than any physical restraint.

And statistically, leaving is the most dangerous time. Abusers escalate when they sense they're losing control. Many domestic violence homicides happen when the victim tries to leave or shortly after they've left.

So when you hear a story like mine and think "I would have left sooner," I hope you'll pause. You don't know what you would have done. And the survivors who do leave—

whenever they leave—deserve nothing but respect for finding the strength to escape.

Intergenerational Patterns and Breaking Cycles

Intergenerational trauma is real. Patterns of abuse, addiction, and dysfunction pass from generation to generation—not just through behavior we witness and copy, but through epigenetics, attachment styles, and learned coping mechanisms that become automatic.

Whatever my mother's reasons were, her choices left scars that shaped my own choices. I found myself drawn to chaos because calm felt foreign. I stayed in relationships where abuse felt familiar because I didn't know what healthy looked like. The patterns repeat because, in a twisted way, dysfunction feels like home. Our nervous systems are wired for the familiar, even when the familiar is destroying us.

But here's what the research also shows: these patterns can be interrupted. With awareness, support, and intentional change, cycles can be broken. It's not easy—you're essentially rewiring patterns that have been passed down for generations. But it's possible.

When my father said I would end up like my mother, he was stating a statistical probability. Children of addicts are more likely to become addicts. Children who experience abuse are more likely to find themselves in abusive relationships. The cycles repeat because that's what cycles do.

But probability is not destiny. And my father's words, meant as a warning or maybe a condemnation, became a challenge. A line in the sand. A promise to myself that I would be the one to break the pattern.

Part 3: Finding Meaning in Your Struggle

I want to be careful here. I'm not suggesting that everything happens for a reason or that trauma is secretly a gift. That kind of toxic positivity dismisses real pain and can make people feel worse for struggling.

What I am suggesting is that humans are meaning-making creatures. We can't help it—we look for patterns, for stories, for ways to make sense of what happens to us. And when we can find meaning in our suffering—not gratitude for it, but meaning within it—we become more resilient.

Viktor Frankl, the psychiatrist and Holocaust survivor, wrote extensively about this. He observed that prisoners who could find meaning—in their suffering, in their survival, in something beyond themselves—were more likely to endure. "Those who have a 'why' to live," he wrote, "can bear with almost any 'how.'"

Thomas was my why. For years, he was the only why I had. That was enough to keep me alive, to keep me fighting, to keep me putting one foot in front of the other even when I couldn't see the path.

Later, I would find other reasons to live. I would build a life that felt worth living for its own sake. But in those early years of struggle, Thomas was everything.

Reflection: Your Catalyst Moments

Think about a moment of hardship in your life that ultimately led to growth. It doesn't have to be dramatic or extreme—sometimes the quiet struggles shape us just as profoundly.

What was the situation? What did it force you to learn or become? Looking back, can you see how that struggle shaped who you are today?

This isn't about finding the silver lining or being grateful for hard times. It's about recognizing your own resilience—the ways you've grown, adapted, and survived things you once thought would break you.

You made it through. That matters.

The Science Behind "Move First"

The Science of Finding Meaning in Hardship

Of all the psychology I've encountered, the research on meaning and purpose has affected me most deeply. Because it answers the question that haunted me for years: What's the point of all this suffering? Why keep going when life is so hard?

The science has an answer. And it's not what you might expect.

Viktor Frankl: The Man Who Found Meaning in Hell

Viktor Frankl was an Austrian psychiatrist who survived four Nazi concentration camps, including Auschwitz and Dachau. He lost his wife. His parents. His brother. Nearly everyone he loved was murdered. He was stripped of everything—his profession, his possessions, his identity, his freedom. He witnessed and experienced horrors that most of us cannot imagine.

And from that unimaginable suffering, he developed one of the most influential psychological theories of the twentieth century: logotherapy.

The name comes from the Greek word "logos," which can be translated as "meaning." Logotherapy is based on a single, powerful premise: the primary human drive is not pleasure (as Freud believed) or power (as Adler believed), but meaning. We are fundamentally meaning-seeking creatures. And we can endure almost anything if we can find meaning in it.

In his landmark book "Man's Search for Meaning," which has sold over 16 million copies and been translated into dozens of languages, Frankl wrote:

"Those who have a 'why' to live can bear with almost any 'how.'"

He was quoting Nietzsche, but he had proved it with his own life. In the camps, Frankl observed that prisoners who had something to live for—a loved one waiting for them, a creative work left unfinished, a purpose they hadn't yet fulfilled—were more likely to survive. Not because they were physically stronger or better fed, but because they had a reason to keep going. They had a "why."

Frankl watched prisoners who lost their sense of meaning simply give up and die. Sometimes within days. Once the inner light went out—once they could no longer find any reason to endure—their bodies followed their spirits.

But he also watched prisoners who, against all logic, maintained or even discovered meaning in the midst of hell. Some found meaning in the hope of reuniting with loved ones. Some found it in the determination to bear witness to what was happening. Some found it in the simple decision to maintain their dignity, to remain human in inhuman circumstances.

Frankl himself survived partly because he was reconstructing a manuscript about logotherapy that the Nazis had confiscated. He wrote on scraps of paper, holding onto his life's work, holding onto meaning.

But here's what struck me most deeply about Frankl's insights:

"Everything can be taken from a man but one thing: the last of human freedoms---to choose one's attitude in any given set of circumstances, to choose one's own way."

Even in Auschwitz. Even with no control over external circumstances. Even facing death at any moment. Frankl insisted that humans retain the power to choose their internal response. This is the ultimate freedom, and it cannot be taken away.

This is a radical statement. And it's the philosophical foundation of "move first. The feeling catches up."

We often feel like victims of our circumstances. We believe that our situation determines our response. That our past dictates our future. That our feelings control our actions. But Frankl, from the most extreme circumstances imaginable, demonstrated that this isn't true. Between stimulus and response, there is a space. In that space lies our power to choose. In that choice lies our growth and our freedom.

Thomas was my why. For years, he was the only why I had. When I wanted to give up, when the pain seemed unbearable, when I couldn't find any reason to keep fighting for myself, I could always find a reason to keep fighting for him. He gave my suffering meaning—the meaning of a mother protecting her child, building a better life for her son.

Later, I found additional meanings. The meaning of using my pain to help other struggling kids. The meaning of breaking generational cycles. The meaning of writing this book. But Thomas was the first why that kept me alive long enough to discover the others.

Frankl also taught something else crucial: meaning cannot be given to us. It must be discovered by each person, in their own way, in their own circumstances. No one can tell you what your life means. You have to find it yourself. But it's there to be found—if you look for it.

Post-Traumatic Growth: The Other Side of Trauma

For decades, psychology focused almost exclusively on the damage that trauma causes. Post-traumatic stress disorder, depression, anxiety, dissociation—the research documented all the ways trauma can shatter lives.

But starting in the 1990s, researchers began noticing something unexpected: some trauma survivors didn't just recover. They grew. They emerged from their suffering stronger, wiser, more compassionate, more alive than they had been before.

Psychologists Richard Tedeschi and Lawrence Calhoun at the University of North Carolina Charlotte coined the term "post-traumatic growth" to describe this phenomenon. Their research has documented five areas where people commonly experience growth after trauma:

Personal strength: Survivors often discover capabilities they didn't know they had. "If I can survive that, I can survive anything."

New possibilities: Trauma can shake people out of old patterns and open them to new paths they never would have considered otherwise.

Relating to others: Many survivors report deeper, more meaningful relationships after trauma—greater empathy, greater capacity for intimacy, greater appreciation for connection.

Appreciation of life: The confrontation with suffering often leads to a profound appreciation for what remains, for small pleasures, for being alive at all.

Spiritual or existential change: Trauma frequently prompts people to grapple with big questions about meaning, purpose, and faith—and to develop deeper or transformed beliefs.

Here's what's crucial to understand: post-traumatic growth doesn't mean trauma is good, or that suffering is necessary for growth, or that people should be grateful for their pain. Trauma is terrible. It causes real damage. Many people are devastated by it and never fully recover.

But the research shows that growth is possible. Not guaranteed—possible. And the possibility is important because it means trauma doesn't have to be the end of the story. The wound can also be the opening.

Tedeschi and Calhoun found that growth typically occurs not instead of distress, but alongside it. People can be simultaneously struggling with the aftermath of trauma and growing from it. The pain doesn't disappear; it coexists with transformation.

They also found that certain factors make post-traumatic growth more likely: social support, the ability to find meaning in the experience, active coping rather than avoidance, and—crucially—taking action to rebuild one's life.

This brings us back to "move first. The feeling catches up." You don't grow from trauma by waiting passively for healing to happen. You grow by engaging with life, by taking action, by actively constructing meaning from your experience. The growth happens through the doing.

Angela Duckworth and the Science of Grit

Dr. Angela Duckworth is a professor at the University of Pennsylvania and the recipient of a MacArthur "genius" grant. She's spent her career asking a simple question: What makes people succeed in the face of adversity?

Her answer: grit.

Grit is passion and perseverance for long-term goals. It's not talent. It's not IQ. It's not any fixed quality you're born with. It's the willingness to keep going when everything in you wants to quit. It's sustained commitment to something that matters to you, maintained over years despite setbacks, obstacles, and the inevitable desire to give up.

Duckworth's research has shown that grit predicts success across an remarkable range of domains.

At West Point, she tracked more than 11,000 cadets through "Beast Barracks"—seven weeks of brutal physical and mental challenges designed to test limits. The attrition rate is typically around 5%. Duckworth found that grit—not physical fitness, not IQ, not SAT scores, not leadership potential as rated by admissions officers—was the best predictor of who would make it through.

In the National Spelling Bee, grittier competitors practiced more, competed more, and ultimately performed better.

In sales, grittier salespeople made more calls and closed more deals.

In tough Chicago schools, grittier students were more likely to graduate.

In every domain Duckworth studied, grit mattered more than talent.

She developed a formula that captures her findings:

Talent × Effort = Skill Skill × Effort = Achievement

Notice that effort appears twice. Talent is the starting point, but effort is what transforms talent into skill. And then effort again is what transforms skill into achievement. Effort counts twice.

This matters enormously because many of us—especially trauma survivors—believe we're not talented enough, smart enough, good enough to succeed. We look at our deficits and conclude we're doomed before we start.

But Duckworth's research shows that effort matters more than talent. And effort is something you can control. You might not be able to change your IQ or your natural aptitude. But you can always control how much effort you put in. You can always choose to try again.

"Our potential is one thing," Duckworth writes. *"What we do with it is quite another."*

Every time I showed up for class despite feeling like I didn't belong, I was building grit. Every time I kept going despite exhaustion and self-doubt, I was proving that effort counts twice. Every time I chose to "move first" despite wanting to quit, I was developing the quality that matters most for long-term success.

Grit isn't something you either have or don't have. It's something you build, choice by choice, day by day. Every time you persist when you want to give up, you become grittier. Every time you "move first," you're strengthening your capacity for grit.

Putting It Into Practice: Building Meaning

How do you actually apply these insights about meaning, growth, and grit to your own life?

Find your why. What gets you out of bed? What would you endure suffering for? It might be a person, a purpose, a principle. It might be large or small. But having a why—even just one—provides an anchor when everything else is chaos.

Look for growth. Not to minimize your pain or pretend everything happens for a reason, but to stay open to the possibility that you might emerge from this stronger. What have you learned? What capacities have you developed? How has your suffering shaped you in ways that might ultimately serve you?

Practice grit. Remember that effort counts twice. When you want to quit, ask yourself: what would it look like to persist just a little longer? What would it mean to keep going, even imperfectly, even slowly?

Choose your attitude. You can't always control what happens to you. But you can always—always—choose your response. In the space between stimulus and response lies your freedom.

Remember that meaning is found through action. You don't discover your purpose by thinking about it in the abstract. You discover it by trying things, by engaging with life, by doing. Meaning emerges from the doing.

Reflection Questions

What is your "why"? What gives your life meaning, even in the hardest times?

Can you identify any areas of post-traumatic growth in your own life? Ways that you've become stronger, wiser, or more compassionate because of what you've survived?

Where in your life have you demonstrated grit—perseverance over long periods toward something that mattered to you?

Viktor Frankl said we always have the freedom to choose our attitude. What attitude do you want to choose toward your current challenges?

What meaning have you made—or could you make—from your hardship?

CHAPTER 4
TRUST
Move First... Even When You're Terrified to Try Again

Part 1: My Story

I was eighteen years old, recently escaped from an abusive relationship, with a baby on my hip and walls around my heart ten feet thick.

I wasn't looking for love. I wasn't looking for anything except survival. Each day was about making it to the next one—working, keeping Thomas fed, staying one step ahead of the chaos that had defined my entire life.

And then there was Jose.

He was thirty-two years old. Patient. Steady. The kind of man who showed up consistently, day after day, without demanding anything in return. In my experience, men always wanted something. They always had an angle. But Jose just... showed up.

I didn't trust it. Of course I didn't. Trust had been beaten out of me long before I met him. Every instinct I had screamed that this was a trap, that he would reveal his true self eventually, that the kindness was just a prelude to something worse.

But here's what made him different from anyone I'd ever known: he fell in love with Thomas first.

Not me. My son.

He didn't try to win me over by being charming or romantic or saying all the right things. He won me over by being good to my child. By playing with Thomas when I was exhausted. By showing up for Thomas when Thomas's biological father never did. By proving, through actions not words, that he could be trusted with the most precious thing in my world.

It took six months before I let my walls down enough to really let him in. Six months of him being patient when I pushed him away. Six months of him not taking it personally when my trauma made me difficult. Six months of him not pushing, not demanding, not trying to rush me past my pain.

He just kept showing up.

That's what love looked like when it didn't hurt. Patience. Consistency. Choosing us—me and Thomas—every single day, even when choosing us was hard.

There wasn't one exact moment I knew I could trust him. It was a slow accumulation of evidence, gathered over months of watching him show up.

I wasn't easy to love. I pushed him away constantly—testing him, waiting for him to reveal himself as just another person who would hurt me. Some days I wanted to try a relationship; other days I played hard to get, convinced that keeping him at arm's length was the only way to protect myself. I gave him every reason to walk away.

But here's the thing: no matter what I did, no matter how hot and cold I ran, no matter how many walls I threw up between us—Jose never stopped showing up for Thomas.

He didn't come around just to see me. He came to see my son. When I pushed him away, he still asked about Thomas. When I told him I wasn't ready, he still wanted to spend time with Thomas. When I was distant and difficult and determined to prove that he'd eventually abandon us like everyone else had, he just kept coming back.

For Thomas. Always for Thomas.

That consistency broke me open in ways I didn't expect. I had never known a man who showed up without an agenda, who kept his word even when it would have been easier to leave, who proved through months of action that he meant what he said.

He fell in love with my son before he fell in love with me. And that's exactly how I knew he was different.

Maybe love didn't have to hurt. Maybe there were people in the world who showed up and stayed. Maybe I was allowed to have this.

The Truth About Our Love Story

I need to be honest with you about something, because I don't want you to read this book and think Jose and I have some perfect fairy tale romance. We don't.

Jose isn't perfect. He has his own trauma, his own struggles, his own stuff he's working through. That's not my story to tell—it's his. But what I can tell you is this: we are not two healed people who found each other and lived happily ever after.

We're two broken people who decided to grow together. Sometimes at different paces. Sometimes in different directions. But always, ultimately, toward each other.

There were years when we drank too much together. There were years when my unprocessed trauma made me push him away so hard I'm amazed he didn't leave. There were moments of frustration and disappointment and wondering if we'd made a mistake.

But we kept choosing each other. That's the real love story.

What it took me a long time to understand is this: I don't want him to be anyone other than who he already is. For years, I confused love with effort—thinking that loving someone meant guiding them, pushing them, helping them become more. But real love isn't about reshaping someone into a different version. It's about seeing them clearly and choosing them anyway. I love him not for who he might become, but for who he is, exactly as he stands. And learning that changed the way I love entirely.

What I CAN do is work on myself. Share my journey. Model what growth looks like. Be a positive influence without making it my mission to change anyone.

Over time, what has changed isn't him becoming someone else—it's his awareness. He can name his trauma now. He can see how his past still echoes into the present. That may sound small, but it isn't. Awareness is the doorway most people never reach.

Change doesn't always look dramatic. Sometimes it looks like recognition. Sometimes it looks like honesty. Sometimes it looks like not turning away anymore.

That's what real love looks like. Not two perfect people. Two imperfect people who keep choosing each other anyway—while giving each other space to grow at their own pace.

I've grown faster than him in some ways. That used to frustrate me. Now I understand: his journey is his. Mine is mine. We walk beside each other, not in lockstep.

And that's enough. That's more than enough.

Part 2: Understanding Intent and Purpose

The Man Who Found Meaning in Suffering

Viktor Frankl was an Austrian psychiatrist who survived the Holocaust. He lost his wife, his parents, his brother—nearly everyone he loved. He spent years in concentration camps, witnessing horrors that most of us can't imagine.

And yet, from that unimaginable suffering, he developed one of the most influential psychological theories of the twentieth century: logotherapy, the idea that the primary human drive is not pleasure (as Freud believed) or power (as Adler believed), but meaning.

"Those who have a 'why' to live," Frankl wrote, "can bear with almost any 'how.'"

In the camps, Frankl observed that prisoners who had something to live for—a loved one waiting for them, a creative work left unfinished, a purpose they hadn't yet fulfilled—were more likely to survive. Not because they were physically stronger, but because they had a reason to keep going.

Purpose matters. Meaning matters. Having a "why" matters.

For me, Thomas was my why. For years, he was the only why I had. When I wanted to give up, when the weight of my trauma felt too heavy to carry, when I couldn't find a single reason to keep fighting for myself—I could always find a reason to keep fighting for him.

Intent vs. Intention: A Crucial Difference

There's a difference between intention and intent, and it took me years to understand it.

Intention is what you plan to do. It's surface-level. "I intend to go to the gym." "I intend to stop drinking." "I intend to be a better parent." Intentions are easy to make and easy to break. They live in the realm of should and someday.

Intent is deeper. Intent is the underlying purpose that drives your actions even when motivation fades. Intent is the why behind the what. Intent doesn't ask "What do I want to do?" It asks "Who do I want to become?"

When I escaped my abusive relationship, I didn't have intentions—those felt too fragile, too likely to fail. What I had was intent. The bone-deep determination that I would not let my son grow up the way I did. That I would break the cycle, whatever it took.

Intent carried me through the nights when I was so tired I couldn't think. It carried me through the moments when giving up seemed easier than going on. It carried me through years of struggle before I saw any evidence that things would get better.

Intentions are what we make on New Year's Eve. Intent is what we live by.

Finding Your Why

Your why doesn't have to be another person. That's what mine was for a long time, but relying solely on external motivation can be dangerous. People leave. People disappoint. People grow up and move out and start their own lives.

Eventually, you need to find a why that includes yourself. A reason to live that doesn't depend on someone else's presence or approval.

For me, that came later. As I healed, I discovered that I wanted to become a school psychologist—to help kids like me, kids whose behavior everyone else saw as problematic but who I recognized as wounded. That became a new why. A purpose beyond survival.

Your why might be creative work that only you can make. It might be justice you want to see in the world. It might be healing itself—becoming whole so that your wholeness can touch others.

It doesn't have to be noble or impressive. It just has to be real. It just has to matter to you.

Part 3: Claiming Your Purpose

Purpose isn't something you find like a lost set of keys. It's something you create, something that emerges from the intersection of your experiences, your values, and your unique way of being in the world.

Sometimes purpose finds you through pain. The thing you suffered through becomes the thing you're uniquely equipped to help others survive. That's not romanticizing trauma—that's transforming it. Taking what was meant to destroy you and using it to build something meaningful.

I didn't choose to be abandoned. I didn't choose abuse or addiction or trauma. But I can choose what I do with those experiences. I can choose to let them define me as a victim, or I can choose to let them equip me as a healer.

That's the power of intent. Not that you can control what happens to you, but that you can control what you do with what happens to you.

Reflection: Finding Your Why

Take some time to reflect on these questions:

What is your "why"? The thing that keeps you going even when everything feels impossible? It doesn't have to be big or noble. It just has to be real.

If you don't have a clear why right now, that's okay. What might it be? What makes you feel alive? What would you fight for?

What's the difference between your intentions (what you plan to do) and your intent (who you want to become)?

Sometimes purpose reveals itself slowly, through the doing. You don't have to have it all figured out. You just have to keep moving.

The Science Behind "Move First"

The Science of Intent and Action

There's a difference between intending to do something and actually doing it. We've all experienced this gap—the distance between our good intentions and our actual behavior. But psychology has revealed both why this gap exists and how to close it.

Peter Gollwitzer and Implementation Intentions

Dr. Peter Gollwitzer is a professor of psychology at New York University who has spent decades studying what he calls the "intention-behavior gap"—the frustrating distance between what we mean to do and what we actually do.

We've all been there. We intend to exercise more, but we don't. We intend to eat healthier, but we don't. We intend to work on our goals, but somehow the days slip by without progress. Why?

Gollwitzer discovered that traditional goal-setting—"I want to exercise more"—often isn't enough. The intention is there, but it's too vague to translate into action. When should you exercise? Where? What kind of exercise? When these questions aren't answered in advance, we have to make decisions in the moment. And moment-to-moment decisions are vulnerable to distraction, fatigue, competing priorities, and simple forgetfulness.

The solution? Implementation intentions.

An implementation intention is a specific plan that takes the form: "If situation X arises, then I will perform behavior Y."

Instead of "I want to exercise more," an implementation intention would be: "If it is 7am on a weekday morning, then I will put on my running shoes and go for a 20-minute run."

Instead of "I want to eat healthier," it would be: "If I am ordering at a restaurant, then I will choose the salad instead of fries."

Instead of "I want to work on my book," it would be: "If I have finished my morning coffee, then I will sit down and write for 30 minutes."

The research on implementation intentions is striking. In a meta-analysis of 94 studies involving over 8,000 participants, Gollwitzer and his colleagues found that implementation intentions had a medium-to-large effect on goal attainment. People who formed specific if-then plans were significantly more likely to follow through than those who just stated their intentions.

Why does this work? Because it delegates control from conscious deliberation to environmental cues. When the situation arises—7am on a weekday—the behavior becomes almost automatic. You don't have to decide whether to exercise. You've already decided. The cue triggers the behavior without requiring willpower in the moment.

This is why Jose's consistency meant so much to me, even before I understood the psychology. He didn't just have a vague intention to be a good partner and father. He had something closer to implementation intentions: When Thomas needs something, I will be there. When Sam is struggling, I will show up. When the family needs support, I will provide it. The decision was made in advance. The showing up became automatic.

Gollwitzer's research has another important finding: implementation intentions are especially powerful for people who struggle with self-control or who face difficult circumstances. The more challenging the situation, the more helpful the specific plan. For trauma survivors, whose self-control is often depleted by the ongoing work of managing symptoms and emotions, this is especially valuable.

You don't have to rely on willpower or motivation in the moment. You can make the decision once, in advance, and let the situation trigger the behavior.

Behavioral Activation: Action Before Feeling

Behavioral Activation is one of the most well-researched treatments for depression, with roots going back to Peter Lewinsohn's work in the 1970s and significant development by Christopher Martell and colleagues in the 2000s.

The core principle is elegantly simple: don't wait to feel better to do things. Do things, and you'll start to feel better.

Research shows that depression creates a vicious cycle. When people are depressed, they withdraw from activities— social events, hobbies, exercise, work. This withdrawal makes sense in the moment: nothing feels appealing, everything seems like too much effort. But the withdrawal deepens the depression. With fewer positive experiences, fewer sources of pleasure and accomplishment, mood sinks further. Which leads to more withdrawal. Which leads to worse mood. And around it goes.

Behavioral Activation breaks this cycle by having people engage in activities regardless of how they feel. You don't wait until you feel like seeing friends to schedule a coffee date. You schedule the coffee date, and often find that you feel better afterward. You don't wait until you feel motivated to exercise to go for a walk. You go for a walk, and often find that your motivation increases.

A landmark 1996 study by Neil Jacobson and colleagues compared full cognitive behavioral therapy (which addresses thoughts, beliefs, and behaviors) to behavioral activation alone (which focuses only on changing behavior). The surprising finding? Behavioral activation by itself was just as effective as the full cognitive package. Changing behavior was enough to change mood.

Multiple meta-analyses have since confirmed this finding. Behavioral activation is as effective as antidepressant medication for many people with depression. And it works by a simple mechanism: action changes feeling.

This is the scientific foundation of "move first. The feeling catches up."

When I was in my darkest periods, I didn't wait to feel motivated to get out of bed. I got out of bed anyway, and the motivation often followed. When I didn't feel like going for a walk, I went anyway, and usually felt better afterward. When I didn't feel like engaging with life, I engaged anyway, and slowly my capacity for engagement returned.

The sequence matters. We naturally assume: feel better → do more. But the research shows it actually works the other way: do more → feel better. Action creates the feeling, not the other way around.

The Motivation Myth

This brings us to one of the most damaging myths about change: the belief that motivation must come first.

"I'll start exercising when I feel motivated." "I'll work on my goals when I'm inspired." "I'll make changes when I'm ready."

The research consistently shows that this is backwards. Motivation follows action far more than action follows motivation.

Dr. BJ Fogg at Stanford, whose work we'll explore more later, puts it this way: "Motivation is unreliable." It fluctuates based on mood, sleep, stress, and countless other factors outside our control. If you wait for motivation to act, you'll spend most of your time waiting.

But here's the good news: you don't need motivation to take action. You just need to take action. And then, often, motivation shows up.

This is why implementation intentions are so powerful—they remove the need for motivation in the moment. The decision is made in advance. The cue triggers the behavior. Motivation becomes optional.

It's also why starting small matters so much. You don't need motivation to do something tiny. You don't need to feel ready to take one small step. And that one small step often generates the momentum and motivation for the next step.

Putting It Into Practice: Closing the Gap

How do you actually close the gap between intention and action?

Create implementation intentions. For your most important goals, create specific if-then plans. When will you do it? Where? What will trigger the behavior? Make the decision in advance so you don't have to rely on in-the-moment willpower.

Start before you feel ready. Don't wait for motivation. Don't wait to feel inspired. Don't wait for the perfect moment.

Start now, start small, start imperfect. The feeling will follow the action.

Use behavioral activation. When you're stuck in a downward spiral—the less you do, the worse you feel, the less you do—break it by doing one thing. Anything. A small activity. A brief social connection. A simple task. Action interrupts the cycle.

Build momentum. Success breeds success. One small action makes the next action easier. Stack wins, however tiny, and let them build.

Remember: motivation is a result, not a requirement. You don't need to feel ready to act. You act, and readiness follows.

Reflection Questions

Where is the gap between your intentions and your actions largest?

What implementation intention (if-then plan) could you create for one important goal?

What is one thing you've been waiting to feel ready for that you could start today?

CHAPTER 5
RECOVERY
Move First... Even When You've Hit Rock Bottom

Part 1: My Story

Our drinking was a secret.

Not many people knew how bad it had gotten. We didn't go to bars—we drank at home, behind closed doors, in the privacy of our own dysfunction. From the outside, we probably looked like a normal couple. From the inside, we were drowning.

It started as a weekend thing. Friday night, crack open a bottle or beers. Saturday, sleep in hungover, then start drinking again to take the edge off. Sunday, recover just enough to face Monday. Rinse and repeat.

But weekends have a way of expanding when you're using alcohol to cope. Friday night became Thursday night because the week had been hard. Sunday drinking bled into Monday because we were already in the habit. Before I fully realized what had happened, we weren't just weekend drinkers anymore.

We were drinking every day.

Every single day. Weekdays, weekends, holidays—it didn't matter. The bottle was always there, and we were always reaching for it.

The Arguments

We argued constantly. About everything. About nothing.

That's what alcohol does to a relationship—it takes every small irritation and magnifies it into a crisis. The dishes in the sink became a screaming match. A misunderstood text became evidence of betrayal. Nothing was ever just nothing; everything was loaded with meaning and accusation and years of unprocessed pain.

At first, I didn't understand what we were really fighting about. It felt like we were arguing about the grocery list or whose turn it was to do something or why he said that thing that way. Surface-level stuff that shouldn't have mattered but somehow did.

But as time went on, the real issues started bleeding through. We weren't arguing about dishes—we were arguing about trauma. My trauma, his trauma, the ways our wounds rubbed against each other and created friction we couldn't name.

And underneath all of it, for me, was trust.

I didn't trust him. Not fully. Not the way you're supposed to trust a partner after years together. My trauma had taught me that people leave, people lie, people hurt you when you're not expecting it. And no matter how many times Jose showed up, no matter how consistent he was, some part of me was always waiting for the other shoe to drop.

So I looked for evidence of betrayal everywhere. I interpreted innocent things as suspicious. I picked fights because fighting felt safer than trusting. At least when we were fighting, I knew what to expect.

The alcohol made all of this worse. It lowered our inhibitions, sure, but it also lowered our defenses against our own worst impulses. Things we might have thought but not said when sober came pouring out after a few drinks. Words we couldn't take back. Accusations we didn't fully mean but couldn't fully deny either.

We were two wounded people, self-medicating with the same poison, wondering why we kept hurting each other.

Rock Bottom

I don't remember much about that time. That's what darkness does—it swallows everything, including memory. What I have are fragments, impressions, the vague outline of days that blurred together into one long nightmare.

What I remember is this: sleeping all day. Not restful sleep—the heavy, drugged unconsciousness of someone trying to escape being awake. I'd surface sometime in the afternoon, groggy and disoriented, already dreading the hours ahead.

I'd eat something—nothing good, nothing that nourished me. Fast food, junk, whatever required the least effort. Food wasn't about health or pleasure anymore; it was just fuel to keep my body functioning while my mind was somewhere else entirely.

Then the drinking would start.

By evening, I'd be deep into several beers, and by night, I'd be fighting with Jose. Fighting about nothing. Fighting about everything. My demons had his face, and I couldn't tell the difference between the man in front of me and the ghosts I was really battling. I blamed him for things that weren't his fault. I pushed him away when all he was trying to do was help.

He knew something was wrong. He could see me drowning. But he didn't know how deep the water was. He didn't know the full extent of what was happening inside my head, the places my thoughts were going when the lights went out.

He tried to be there for me. He really did. But how do you help someone who keeps shoving you away? How do you save someone who seems determined to sink? My pushing became too much for him at some points. He didn't know how to help, and I didn't know how to let him.

Sleep. Eat badly. Drink. Fight. Repeat.

That was my life. Day after day after day. COVID had trapped us all inside, and I was trapped inside something even smaller—the prison of my own mind, with walls closing in tighter every day.

The Darkness

There were nights I didn't want to exist anymore.

I need to be honest about that, even though it's hard to write. Even though part of me wants to skip over this part and pretend it didn't happen. It happened. It was real. And if someone reading this is in that same dark place right now, I need them to know they're not alone.

Some nights, when the drinking had taken me past the point of rational thought, I tried to make sure I wouldn't wake up. I won't go into details—that's not helpful for anyone. But I need you to understand how dark it got. How close I came to not being here to write this book.

By some miracle, I kept waking up.

I don't know why. I don't have a neat explanation or an inspiring story about what pulled me back from the edge. I don't remember a moment of clarity, a turning point, a decision to choose life. That time is a blur—dark and foggy and fragmented.

What I know is that I'm still here. Against all odds, despite my own worst impulses, I kept waking up. And eventually, something shifted. Not dramatically—not a lightning bolt of transformation. Just a slow, gradual crawl out of the pit I'd fallen into.

Maybe it was Jose's persistence, even when I pushed him away. Maybe it was Thomas, even though I wasn't the mother he deserved during that time. Maybe it was some stubborn survival instinct buried so deep I didn't even know it existed. Maybe it was just luck—the same luck that kept me waking up on mornings I'd tried not to.

I don't have answers. I just have the fact of my survival.

And maybe that's enough. Maybe the story doesn't need a tidy resolution or an inspiring turning point. Maybe the miracle is simply this: I was in the darkest place a person can be, and somehow, I made it through to the other side.

If you're in that dark place right now, I'm not going to tell you it gets better. I know how hollow that sounds when you're drowning. What I will tell you is this: I've been there. I've been exactly where you are. And I'm still here.

That's not a promise that you'll feel better tomorrow. It's just proof that survival is possible, even when it doesn't feel like it. Even when you don't want it. Even when you're actively fighting against it.

Sometimes we survive despite ourselves. And sometimes, that's the only kind of survival available.

The Last Fight

I don't remember exactly what the last fight was about. Maybe that's fitting—so many of our arguments were about nothing and everything at the same time.

What I remember is the aftermath. The silence after the screaming. The heaviness of knowing we couldn't keep doing this. The exhaustion—not just physical, but spiritual. Soul-deep tired of living this way.

Something shifted that night. I don't know if it was me or him or both of us at the same time, but we looked at each other and we knew: this had to stop. Not just the fighting—the drinking. The whole toxic cycle we'd built our relationship around.

We chose to stop. Cold turkey. Just like that.

I know that's not how it works for everyone. I know some people need medical supervision to detox safely, need rehab, need programs and sponsors and structured support. We were lucky—or maybe we hadn't gone quite as far down as we thought. Either way, we just... stopped.

And everything changed.

Saturday Mornings

The first Saturday morning we woke up early—really early, without hangovers—felt like stepping into a new world.

We went to the public market. I don't know whose idea it was, or if it was anyone's idea at all. Maybe we just needed to do something different, to fill the space that drinking used to occupy with something that wouldn't destroy us.

The crisp morning air hit my face and I felt... awake. Actually awake, not the groggy half-consciousness of sleeping off a hangover. My senses were sharper than they'd been in years. I could smell the vendors' coffee brewing, the fresh bread, the flowers at the corner stand. I could hear conversations clearly instead of through the fog of last night's wine.

We walked through the market slowly, no rush, no headaches, no desperate need to find greasy food to settle our stomachs. We bought things we actually wanted to eat—fresh vegetables, good cheese, bread that was still warm. We sat down for breakfast and had a real conversation, not the tense negotiations of two hungover people trying not to snap at each other.

It was magical. That's the only word for it. We had been missing this our entire relationship—these simple, beautiful mornings that sober people take for granted. We'd traded years of Saturdays for hangovers and regret, and we never even knew what we were giving up.

That first Saturday became a ritual. Every week, we'd wake up early and go to the market. Every week, it felt like a gift—this life we'd almost drunk away, given back to us.

Becoming Someone New

I started taking care of myself in ways I never had before.

When I was drinking, I didn't care how I looked. Sweats every day, hair thrown up, no makeup—what was the point? I was just going to end up on the couch with alcohol anyway. My outside matched my inside: neglected, disheveled, barely holding together.

But sober? Sober, I wanted to look good. I started dressing better, putting effort into my appearance, caring about the impression I made on the world. Not for anyone else—for me. Because I was finally someone worth taking care of.

I felt great. I looked great. People started commenting on it—"You're glowing," they'd say. And I was. Happiness will do that to you. Sobriety will do that to you. Waking up without shame will do that to you.

Jose and I started actually talking. Not arguing, not negotiating cease-fires, not having the same circular fights about the same old wounds. Talking. About our lives, our dreams, our fears. About how bad things had gotten and how grateful we were to be on the other side.

We would sit together and marvel at the life we'd almost lost. "Remember when we used to spend every weekend hungover?" one of us would say. "Remember when we argued every single day?" And we'd shake our heads at our past selves, amazed that we'd lived that way for so long, amazed that we'd found our way out.

We made a promise to each other: we would never go back. No matter what happened, no matter how hard things got, we would never return to that life. The bottle had taken enough from us.

I'm glad I'm still here. I'm glad I get to write this book, raise my son, love my husband, walk my dogs in the morning sunlight. I'm glad I get to help other people's kids the way I wished someone had helped me. I'm glad for all of it—even though there were nights I tried to throw it all away.

The darkness didn't win. I don't fully understand why, but it didn't win.

Learning to Say No

The invitations still come. They always will.

"Come out with us! Let's grab drinks! We're going to happy hour—you should come!"

I decline them all. Every single one.

Some people don't understand. They think I'm being antisocial or boring or that I think I'm better than them. I don't explain myself anymore. I don't owe anyone an explanation for protecting my sobriety, my relationship, my life.

The truth is, I know myself. I know that "just one drink" doesn't exist for me. I know that the life I have now—the Saturday mornings, the clear head, the genuine connection with Jose, the energy to pursue my dreams—is worth more than any night out.

We started waking up early. We started walking more, hiking on weekends, building a life around health instead of hangovers. We developed routines that supported who we wanted to be instead of enabling who we'd been.

The feeling of this new life? It felt good. Better than any buzz ever had. This was sustainable happiness, not the temporary escape that always left us worse off than before.

We found each other again in sobriety. Or maybe we found each other for the first time—the real versions of ourselves, not the numbed, defensive, wounded versions that had been stumbling through our relationship for years.

Getting sober didn't fix everything. Jose still has his struggles; I still have mine. But at least now we're facing them clear-eyed, together, without a bottle standing between us.

That's worth more than I can say.

The Ten-Year Degree

It took me ten years to finish my bachelor's degree.

Ten years. A decade of starting and stopping, of registering for classes and then having to drop them, of life getting in the way over and over again.

I'd sign up for a semester, full of hope and determination. This time would be different. This time I'd make it work. And then something would happen—money would get tight, work would demand more mental load, Thomas would need me, life would explode in some new and unexpected way—and I'd have to stop again.

Each time I stopped, the voice in my head had something to say about it. See? You can't even finish college. You're never going to amount to anything. Who did you think you were, trying to get a degree?

But each time, eventually, I'd start again.

I'd let a semester pass, maybe two, maybe a whole year. I'd lick my wounds and deal with whatever crisis had derailed me. And then I'd pull out the course catalog again, fill out the registration forms, and try one more time.

That's the part nobody talks about when they celebrate someone's graduation. They don't see the five times you almost quit. They don't see the semesters you couldn't afford textbooks, the nights you stayed up studying after a full day of work, the tears you cried in your car in the parking lot because you were so tired and it all felt so impossible.

They just see the diploma. They don't see the decade of struggle behind it.

The Juggle

During those years, I was working full-time. I was raising Thomas. I was navigating my relationship with Jose through all its ups and downs. I was getting sober. I was trying to become a person I could be proud of.

And somewhere in the margins of all that, I was also trying to get an education.

I took classes whenever I could fit them in. Online classes at midnight after Thomas went to bed. Weekend classes that ate into the only free time I had. Summer intensives that left me exhausted but a few credits closer to the finish line.

Some semesters I could only afford one class. Some semesters I had to choose between tuition and groceries. Some semesters the financial aid didn't come through in time and I had to scramble to figure out how to pay or take out loans.

It was never easy. It was never convenient. There was never a "good time" to go back to school—I just had to make time, steal time from sleep and self-care and everything else, and hope it would be enough.

People would say things like, "I don't know how you do it all." And I'd smile and shrug, because the truth was too complicated to explain. The truth was: I'm barely holding it together. The truth was: Most days I feel like I'm failing at everything. The truth was: I don't know how I do it either; I just don't have another choice.

Graduation

In 2025, at thirty-five years old, I finally graduated with my bachelor's degree in Psychology.

I accepted my diploma, and I thought about all the times I'd almost given up. All the semesters I'd had to withdraw. All the nights I'd cried because it felt impossible. All the people who probably thought I'd never finish.

I did it anyway.

Ten years. Countless setbacks. A whole lifetime of chaos and trauma and reasons to quit. And I still made it to that stage.

That diploma represents so much more than education. It represents persistence. It represents refusing to give up on myself, even when giving up would have been easier. It represents proving wrong every voice—internal and external—that said I couldn't do it.

If you're reading this and you're in the middle of your own ten-year journey—whatever that journey is—I want you to know: it's okay that it's taking longer than you planned. It's okay that you've had to stop and start. It's okay that your path doesn't look like anyone else's.

What matters is that you keep coming back. What matters is that you don't let the setbacks become the end of the story.

I'm living proof that you can finish things a decade later than planned and still have it mean everything.

What Now?

Here's where I'm supposed to tell you about my clear vision for the future. The master's degree I'm pursuing with passion and certainty. The career path I've mapped out. The next chapter all neatly planned.

But I promised to be honest in this book, so here's the truth: I'm not sure.

I'm currently in graduate school for School Psychology. I've also been accepted to an MSW program. I'm pursuing advanced degrees because that's what you're supposed to do, right? Because you can't do anything in the helping professions without a master's or a license or some official credential that says you're qualified to do what you've already been doing for fifteen years.

But if I'm being honest? I don't want to work for a company. I don't want to sit in an office somewhere, following someone else's rules, fitting into someone else's system. I've done that. I've given fifteen years of my life to school districts, and I burned out so badly I had to resign.

What I want is to help people on my own terms.

I started Compass Behavior Support because I wanted to work directly with families, to provide the kind of guidance and support that I wished someone had given me when I was struggling. I wanted to take everything I've learned—professionally and personally—and use it to help others navigate the chaos of raising kids with challenging behaviors.

That's the dream. That's what lights me up.

The graduate degree? If I'm being completely honest, it's my fallback. It's the credential I'm getting just in case—just in case the business doesn't work, just in case I need to go back to a traditional job, just in case I need the letters after my name to be taken seriously.

I don't know if that's the right approach. I don't know if I'm wasting time and money on a degree I might never use, or if I'm being smart by having a backup plan. I don't have it all figured out.

And maybe that's okay.

Maybe part of being thirty-five and still figuring things out is accepting that you don't need to have all the answers. Maybe the path will become clearer as I walk it. Maybe the uncertainty is just part of the journey.

What I know for sure is this: I want to help people. I want to use my experience—all of it, the trauma and the recovery and the professional training—to make a difference in people's lives. How exactly that will look, I'm still figuring out.

But I've spent my whole life figuring things out as I go. Why stop now?

Part 2: The Reality of Recovery

Why Willpower Alone Doesn't Work

If willpower were enough, everyone who wanted to change would change. But research shows that willpower is a limited resource—it depletes throughout the day, it's weakened by stress, and it's virtually useless against deeply ingrained habits.

This isn't a character flaw. It's neuroscience. Habits live in a different part of the brain than conscious decisions. Once a behavior becomes habitual, it operates on autopilot, requiring little to no conscious thought. That's why you can drive a familiar route without remembering the journey, and it's why you can find yourself pouring a drink without deciding to.

Changing deeply rooted behaviors requires more than deciding to change. It requires understanding your triggers, modifying your environment, building new neural pathways, and having systems in place for when willpower fails—because it will.

The Stages of Change

Psychologists James Prochaska and Carlo DiClemente developed the Transtheoretical Model, which describes how people move through stages when making behavioral changes:

Precontemplation: You don't see a problem, or you're not ready to address it. ("I can stop whenever I want. I just don't want to.")

Contemplation: You're aware there's a problem and you're thinking about changing, but you haven't committed yet. ("Maybe I should cut back... but not today.")

Preparation: You're getting ready to change. You're making plans, gathering resources, setting a start date. ("I'm going to stop after the holidays.")

Action: You're actively changing the behavior. This is the stage most people think of as "recovery." ("I haven't had a drink in three weeks.")

Maintenance: The new behavior has become part of your life. You're working to prevent relapse and solidify the change. ("I've been sober for a year and it feels natural now.")

Here's what's important to know: most people cycle through these stages multiple times before change sticks. Relapse isn't failure—it's part of the process. Each attempt teaches you something. Each fall gives you information about what doesn't work, which gets you closer to what does.

I cycled through these stages more times than I can count. I "decided" to stop drinking dozens of times before I actually stopped. Each failed attempt felt like proof that I couldn't change. But looking back, I can see that each attempt was practice. Each one got me a little closer.

What Actually Works

Research on behavior change points to several factors that increase the likelihood of success:

Environment design: Make the healthy choice the easy choice. Remove triggers from your environment. If you don't want to drink, don't keep alcohol in the house. If you want to exercise, put your gym clothes out the night before. Your environment shapes your behavior more than your willpower does.

Social support: Change is easier when you're not doing it alone. Find people who support your goals—friends, family, support groups, therapists. Having Jose on this journey with me made an enormous difference.

Replacement behaviors: You can't just remove a behavior; you have to replace it with something else. Drinking was how I relaxed, how I socialized, how I coped with stress. I needed new ways to do all those things—hiking, yoga, walking the dogs, calling a friend.

Self-compassion: This might be the most important one. Research shows that people who treat themselves with kindness after setbacks are more likely to try again than people who beat themselves up. Shame doesn't motivate change; it paralyzes it.

Part 3: Building Your Recovery Toolkit

Recovery—from addiction, from trauma, from any pattern that's holding you back—isn't a destination. It's an ongoing practice. You don't recover once and then you're done. You recover daily, sometimes hourly, one choice at a time.

What you need is a toolkit—a set of strategies, supports, and resources you can draw on when things get hard. Not a perfect plan, but a collection of options. Because some days, the thing that works is a phone call to a friend, and other days it's a walk around the block, and other days it's just going to bed early so you don't have to fight the urge anymore.

Reflection: Your Recovery Toolkit

Consider these questions as you build your own toolkit:

Who can you call when you're struggling? Make a list of people who support your growth—not people who enable old patterns.

What activities help you feel grounded? What can you do instead of the behavior you're trying to change?

What environments or situations trigger you? How can you avoid them, or prepare for them if you can't avoid them?

What's one small change you could make this week? Not the whole transformation—just one small step.

Remember: you don't have to be perfect. You just have to keep trying. Keep getting back up. Keep choosing differently, one moment at a time.

The Science Behind "Move First"

The Science of Rebuilding

Recovery isn't a straight line. It's not a single dramatic moment of transformation. It's built—brick by brick, day by day, choice by choice. And the science of behavior change shows us exactly how this building happens.

BJ Fogg and Tiny Habits

Dr. BJ Fogg founded the Behavior Design Lab at Stanford University and has spent over twenty years studying what makes behavior change stick. His conclusion might seem counterintuitive at first: if you want to change your life, make it tiny.

Most behavior change fails because we try to do too much too fast. We're motivated on January 1st, so we commit to exercising every day, eating perfectly healthy, meditating for an hour, and writing in our journals. By January 15th, we've abandoned all of it.

The problem isn't lack of willpower. The problem is design.

When we set big goals that require high motivation, we're setting ourselves up for failure. Motivation is unreliable—it surges and crashes based on factors outside our control. If your success depends on feeling motivated every day, you won't succeed. Because you won't feel motivated every day.

Fogg's solution: make the behavior so tiny that motivation barely matters.

Instead of "I'll exercise for an hour," try "I'll do two pushups."

Instead of "I'll meditate for 30 minutes," try "I'll take three deep breaths."

Instead of "I'll write in my journal every day," try "I'll write one sentence."

These behaviors are so small that you can do them even when motivation is at zero. Even on your worst day, you can do two pushups. Even when you're exhausted, you can take three breaths. Even when you don't feel like writing, you can write one sentence.

But here's what Fogg discovered: tiny habits establish the pattern. And patterns can grow.

Once you're doing two pushups every day without fail, you naturally start doing three, then five, then ten. Once you're taking three breaths every morning, you naturally start extending it. The tiny habit is the seed; growth happens naturally once the seed is planted.

Fogg identifies three elements necessary for any behavior: motivation, ability, and prompt.

Motivation is the desire to do the behavior.

Ability is the capacity to do it—how easy or hard it is.

Prompt is the trigger that reminds you to do it.

When a behavior doesn't happen, it's because one of these elements is missing. Maybe you have the motivation but not the ability (the behavior is too hard). Maybe you have the ability but no prompt (you simply forget). Maybe you have the prompt but no motivation (you're reminded but don't care).

Most people try to fix behavior change by increasing motivation—pumping themselves up, setting inspiring goals, visualizing success. But motivation is the least reliable element. It's far more effective to increase ability (make the behavior easier) and improve prompts (link the behavior to something you already do).

This transformed my approach to recovery. Instead of trying to overhaul my entire life at once, I started with tiny changes:

One morning walk—not an hour of exercise, just one walk. One glass of water before coffee—not a complete diet overhaul, just one glass. One moment of gratitude—not a whole journaling practice, just one moment.

Those tiny habits accumulated. They grew. They became the foundation of a completely different life.

Fogg also emphasizes something crucial: "You change best by feeling good, not by feeling bad."

Shame and guilt are terrible motivators. They might produce a burst of effort, but they don't sustain change. What sustains change is the good feeling of success—the small celebration when you complete your tiny habit, the sense of accomplishment, the growing evidence that you're someone who does this thing.

This is why tiny habits work: they let you succeed easily and often. Each success builds confidence and positive emotion. Each win, however small, reinforces the behavior.

Walter Mischel and Strategic Self-Control

Dr. Walter Mischel is famous for the "marshmallow test"—one of the most well-known experiments in psychology. In the late 1960s at Stanford, Mischel offered young children a choice: one marshmallow now, or two marshmallows if they could wait fifteen minutes.

Then he watched what happened.

Some children grabbed the marshmallow immediately. Others waited, squirming, covering their eyes, sitting on their hands, singing songs—and eventually earned the second marshmallow. Follow-up studies years later found that children who had been able to wait tended to have better life outcomes: higher SAT scores, lower rates of obesity, better ability to handle stress.

The marshmallow test is often presented as evidence that willpower is a fixed trait—either you have self-control or you don't. But that's not what Mischel concluded. His actual findings are far more hopeful.

Mischel discovered that successful delay wasn't about willpower at all. It was about strategy.

The children who waited weren't sitting there white-knuckling their way through temptation. They were using strategies—covering the marshmallow, turning away from it, singing songs to distract themselves, pretending the marshmallow was something else (a cloud, a cotton ball), mentally transforming the situation to make waiting easier.

The children who tried to resist through pure willpower—staring at the marshmallow, trying to force themselves not to eat it—almost always failed.

"Willpower is not something you either have or don't have," Mischel explained in his later writing. *"It's a skill that can be taught and strengthened through specific strategies."*

This has profound implications for recovery. If you're trying to change through willpower alone—through gritting your teeth and forcing yourself to resist—you're setting yourself up for failure. Pure willpower is exhausting and unreliable.

But if you use strategies—changing your environment, creating distance from temptation, transforming how you think about the situation—change becomes much more achievable.

This is why my Saturday morning walks with Jose were so powerful. They weren't about willpower. They were about strategy. We replaced the old Saturday morning trigger (which had been associated with drinking) with a new behavior (walking) that was incompatible with the old one. We changed the environment. We didn't rely on me white-knuckling my way through temptation; we designed a system that made temptation less present.

Strategic self-control means:

Changing your environment to remove temptations or friction Creating "bright line rules" that are absolute (no exceptions means no decisions to make) Using implementation intentions to automate behavior Building routines that make good choices the default Finding alternative sources for whatever the problematic behavior provided

Recovery isn't about having more willpower than other people. It's about being strategic with the willpower you have.

James Clear and Identity-Based Habits

James Clear, author of "Atomic Habits," built on Fogg's and others' research to develop a framework for identity-based behavior change that has helped millions.

Clear distinguishes between three levels of change:

Outcome level: What you want to achieve. "I want to lose weight."

Process level: What you do. "I go to the gym three times a week."

Identity level: Who you are. "I'm the kind of person who takes care of their body."

Most people try to change at the outcome level. They focus on the goal—lose 20 pounds, write a book, get sober. But outcome-based change often fails because you're still the same person trying to achieve a different result.

The most sustainable changes happen at the identity level. When you shift your identity—who you believe yourself to be—your behaviors naturally follow. You don't have to force yourself to go to the gym if you genuinely see yourself as "someone who works out." You don't have to struggle against drinking if you genuinely see yourself as "someone who doesn't drink."

Clear argues that identity is formed through evidence. Every action you take is a vote for the type of person you wish to become. One pushup is a vote for "I'm someone who exercises." One day without drinking is a vote for "I'm someone who is sober." One kind word is a vote for "I'm someone who is compassionate."

No single vote is decisive. But over time, the votes accumulate. The evidence builds. The identity shifts.

This is why tiny habits matter so much: each tiny habit is a vote for your new identity. Each time you do your two pushups, you're casting a vote for "I'm someone who exercises." Each time you do your morning walk, you're voting for "I'm someone who takes care of themselves."

The behaviors build the identity. The identity sustains the behaviors. The cycle reinforces itself.

I'm no longer someone who drank to cope. I'm someone who hikes, who does yoga, who walks dogs at sunrise. That's not a behavior I maintain through willpower—it's who I am now. The votes accumulated. The evidence mounted. The identity solidified.

Putting It Into Practice: Building Sustainable Change

How do you actually apply these findings to rebuild your life?

Start with tiny habits. What is the smallest possible version of the change you want to make? So small you can't say no? Start there. Let it grow naturally.

Focus on the process, then let identity follow. Instead of obsessing about outcomes, focus on showing up and doing the process. Each time you do it, you're voting for a new identity.

Use strategy, not willpower. Don't try to resist temptation through sheer force of will. Change your environment. Create systems. Automate good decisions.

Celebrate small wins. When you complete your tiny habit, feel good about it. That positive emotion reinforces the behavior. Shame and guilt push you away from change; celebration pulls you toward it.

Build evidence for your new identity. Ask yourself: "What would a [healthy/sober/successful/confident] person do?" Then do that thing, however imperfectly. You're not pretending—you're building evidence.

Remember: you change best by feeling good, not by feeling bad. Not through shame, but through celebration. Not through massive overhauls, but through tiny consistent steps.

Reflection Questions

What tiny habit could you start today—the smallest possible version of the change you want?

What environmental changes could make your desired behaviors easier?

What identity are you building through your daily actions?

CHAPTER 6
SELF-COMPASSION
Move First... Even When the Voice Says You Can't

Part 1: My Story

For as long as I can remember, I've had an enemy living inside my head.

She sounds like me, but meaner. She notices every mistake, catalogs every failure, and reminds me of every reason I'm not good enough. When I mess up—even something small—she's right there:

See? Told you. You're not smart enough. You're not pretty enough. You're not enough, period. Who did you think you were, trying to be different?

That voice has been with me since childhood. Maybe since before I can remember. It's the voice that formed in that dark house when I was four, the voice that concluded I must be forgettable, leaveable, not worth staying for. It's the voice that got louder with every trauma, every abandonment, every time someone proved that I wasn't a priority.

For most of my life, I thought that voice was just... me. I thought everyone walked around with a constant internal critic, beating themselves up for every imperfection. I didn't realize it was a wound. I didn't realize it could be healed.

Learning self-compassion has been one of the hardest parts of my healing journey. Because you can't be kind to yourself if you don't believe you deserve kindness. And for thirty-something years, I didn't believe I deserved much of anything.

Starting Small

The shift didn't happen overnight. It couldn't—I was too broken for dramatic transformation. What I could handle was small. Tiny. Almost embarrassingly simple.

I started with yoga, more like "stretching" my body.

I'd always admired people who did yoga—they seemed calm, centered, like they had their lives together in ways I couldn't imagine. But I'd never committed to it myself. Too busy. Too tired. Too convinced I'd be bad at it.

One morning, I sat on the floor in my living room and pulled up a beginner video online. I felt ridiculous. My balance was terrible. My muscles shook in poses that looked effortless to the instructor. I was acutely aware of every limitation, every imperfection, every way my body wasn't cooperating.

But something happened during that first session that surprised me. For five minutes, I wasn't thinking about my trauma. I wasn't replaying old wounds or worrying about the future. I was just... breathing. Stretching. Existing in my body instead of escaping from it.

It wasn't about touching my toes or getting the poses right. It was about showing up for myself. About treating my body like something worth taking care of, even when I didn't fully believe it yet.

I kept going. Not every day at first—some weeks I'd skip more days than I'd show up. But I kept coming back. And slowly, yoga became less about exercise and more about ritual. A daily act of kindness toward a body I'd spent most of my life punishing.

Learning to Sit Still

Then came meditation, and that was even harder.

Sitting still with my own thoughts? For someone with a lifetime of trauma to avoid? It sounded like torture. My brain was not a peaceful place to hang out. It was full of anxiety and self-criticism and memories I'd spent years trying to outrun.

But I'd heard enough about the benefits that I decided to try. Just five minutes a day. How hard could that be?

Really hard, it turns out.

The first few days were brutal. I'd sit down, close my eyes, try to focus on my breath, and within seconds my mind would be racing. Grocery lists. Old arguments. Things I should have said differently. Worries about Thomas. Worries about money. Worries about everything.

And then the voice would chime in: You can't even meditate right. Other people can do this. What's wrong with you?

But I kept trying. I learned that the goal isn't to stop thinking—that's impossible. The goal is to notice when you've drifted and gently bring yourself back. No judgment. No criticism. Just: Oh, I'm thinking about that thing again. Okay. Back to breathing.

That gentleness was revolutionary for me. I had never been gentle with myself about anything. But meditation forced me to practice it, over and over, dozens of times in a single five-minute session. Drift. Notice. Return. No beating myself up about it.

Over weeks, something shifted. I became more patient— not just during meditation, but in my life. I became less reactive, more able to pause before responding. I started noticing my inner critic in real-time, recognizing her voice as something separate from my true self.

Meditation became a daily gift I gave myself. Five minutes of peace in a life that had known so little of it.

My Furry Teachers

And then there are the dogs.

Bruno came first—my soul dog. He's two now, a pit bull with a heart bigger than his massive head. From the moment I met him, something clicked. He looked at me with those eyes, and I felt seen in a way that's hard to explain. Dogs don't care about your trauma or your failures or the voice in your head that says you're not enough. They just love you. Fully. Unconditionally. Without any of the complicated strings that come with human relationships.

Then came Otis and Lyla—our puppies, still babies really. The house is chaos now, in the best possible way. Three pities demanding walks and attention and treats, keeping me grounded in the present moment, whether I want to be or not.

Walking them became another practice of self-compassion, though I didn't recognize it as that at first.

Every morning, no matter how I'm feeling, I take them out. Rain or shine. Good mood or bad. Depressed or energized. The dogs don't care about my mental state—they need to walk, and that need gets me out of bed on days when nothing else could.

Those walks became meditative. I started paying attention to things I'd normally rush past—the way the light hits the trees, the sounds of birds, the feeling of cool air on my face. I'd watch Bruno's pure joy at being outside, the way his whole body wiggled with happiness at the simplest things, and I'd think: Maybe I could learn something from this.

Dogs live completely in the present. They don't ruminate about yesterday or worry about tomorrow. They're just here, now, fully experiencing whatever this moment has to offer. Walking with them taught me to do the same—at least for those thirty minutes each morning.

And there's something about the unconditional love of a dog that heals wounds humans can't reach. Bruno doesn't care about my past. He doesn't know about the dark house or the abuse or the years of drinking. He just knows that I'm his person, and he loves me completely. Being loved like that—

simply, without conditions—taught me something about the kind of love I deserved.

Finding the Language

For a long time, I thought something was wrong with me because I couldn't seem to "get motivated" the way other people did. I waited to feel ready before I acted. I waited to feel confident before I spoke up. I waited to feel deserving before I tried. And while I waited, my life stayed exactly the same.

Eventually, I started noticing a pattern. The days I moved my body—even when I didn't want to—I felt better afterward. The days I showed up to class despite feeling out of place, the confidence followed later. The days I did the hard thing first, the fear loosened its grip. Not before. After.

That's when it clicked: motivation wasn't the starting point. It was the result.

I had spent my whole life waiting for a feeling that was never going to arrive on its own. Readiness didn't come first. Courage didn't come first. Confidence didn't come first. Action did. The feeling always caught up later—sometimes slowly, sometimes quietly, but reliably.

Once I saw that, everything shifted.

I stopped arguing with myself. I stopped trying to convince my fear to disappear before I moved. I stopped waiting for my inner critic to quiet down. I learned that I didn't need permission from my emotions to take action. I could move first and let my nervous system adjust afterward.

That realization changed how I approached everything. When I didn't want to work out, I moved anyway. When I didn't want to study, I opened the book anyway. When the voice in my head told me I wasn't capable, I didn't debate it—I acted in spite of it. Each action became evidence. Each step forward weakened the story that said I couldn't.

The more I acted, the less power that voice had.

I didn't suddenly become fearless. I didn't magically feel confident. But I stopped letting feelings dictate my choices. And that was the difference between staying stuck and starting to build a life.

Because here's the truth I had to learn the hard way: I was never incapable. I was never lazy. I was never broken. I had already done hard things. I had survived things that should have destroyed me. I just forgot that survival had already proven my strength.

Action reminded me.

That's where Move First came from. Not from a podcast. Not from a quote. From lived experience. From testing the idea again and again in real life and watching it work. The feeling always catches up. Not instantly. Not perfectly. But enough to keep going.

And once you see that pattern, you can't unsee it.

The Mirror

And then there's the high-five habit.

I'm going to be honest: it felt absolutely ridiculous at first.

The idea is simple: every morning, you look at yourself in the mirror and give your reflection a high-five. That's it. Just a physical gesture of self-encouragement, a way of telling yourself "good job" before the day has even started.

The first time I tried it, I felt like an idiot. I stood in my bathroom, looked at my tired reflection, and raised my hand to the mirror. It felt forced. Fake. Like I was playing pretend at self-love.

But I did it anyway.

The next day, still silly. The day after that, still awkward. But I kept doing it, because Mel Robbins said to do it, and I'd decided to trust her process even when it felt stupid.

And then something shifted.

I don't know exactly when it happened—maybe a week in, maybe two. But one morning I looked in the mirror and the high-five didn't feel fake anymore. It felt like acknowledgment. Like recognition. Like I was finally seeing myself the way I'd always seen others—as someone worthy of encouragement, capable of growth, deserving of celebration.

For someone who had spent her entire life being her own worst enemy, this was revolutionary. A high-five. Such a small thing. But it cracked something open in me.

Now I high-five myself every morning without thinking about it. It's just part of my routine, like brushing my teeth or making coffee. A tiny daily act of self-compassion that reminds me: You're doing okay. You're showing up. That matters.

The Voice Gets Quieter

I still have an inner critic. I don't think she ever fully goes away—not when she's been with you since childhood, not when she was formed in trauma and reinforced by years of believing you weren't enough.

But she's quieter now. And there's another voice too—a kinder one. One that says: You got this, Samantha. Everything will work out the way it's supposed to. One that sounds less like criticism and more like encouragement.

When something goes wrong now, I try to pause before the harsh voice takes over. I ask myself: What would I say to a friend in this situation? Would I tell her she's worthless and stupid? Or would I tell her it's okay, mistakes happen, let's figure out what to do next?

I'm learning to be that friend to myself.

It's still hard. Some days the critic wins. Some days I spiral into old patterns of self-blame and shame. But those days are fewer now, and I recover from them faster. The practices I've built—the yoga, the meditation, the walks with my dogs, the high-fives in the mirror—they're like a safety net. Even when I fall, I don't fall as far.

Self-compassion didn't come naturally to me. It had to be learned, practiced, repeated until it started to stick. But it's changing everything—how I treat myself, how I relate to others, how I move through the world.

I'm finally becoming my own friend instead of my own enemy. And that might be the most important transformation of all.

Part 2: The Science of Self-Compassion

What Self-Compassion Actually Is

Dr. Kristin Neff, a pioneering researcher in the field, identifies three core components of self-compassion:

Self-kindness: Treating yourself with warmth and understanding when you suffer, fail, or feel inadequate, rather than ignoring your pain or attacking yourself with self-criticism. This is the opposite of what most of us learned to do. We learned that criticism motivates change, that being hard on ourselves makes us better. Research shows the opposite is true.

Common humanity: Recognizing that suffering and personal inadequacy is part of the shared human experience—something we all go through rather than something that happens to "me" alone. When we fail, we tend to feel isolated, like we're the only ones who struggle this way. But imperfection is universal. Recognizing this connects us to others rather than separating us.

Mindfulness: Holding your pain in balanced awareness rather than over-identifying with it. This means neither suppressing your feelings nor getting swept away by them. You can acknowledge that something hurts without letting that pain define you or consume you.

Self-Compassion vs. Self-Esteem

Self-compassion is not the same as self-esteem, and the difference matters.

Self-esteem is about evaluating yourself positively—feeling special, above average, worthy because of your accomplishments or qualities. The problem is that self-esteem is contingent. It rises when you succeed and falls when you fail. It depends on being better than others, which means it's always at risk.

Self-compassion is different. It doesn't depend on being special or successful. It's about treating yourself with kindness regardless of your performance—whether you succeed or fail, whether you're having a good day or a terrible one. It's stable in a way that self-esteem never can be.

This was crucial for me to understand. My whole life, I'd been chasing self-esteem—trying to prove I was good enough through achievement, through being needed, through external validation. But it never lasted. One failure and I was right back to feeling worthless.

Self-compassion offered something more sustainable: the ability to be okay with myself even when things weren't okay. To treat myself with kindness not because I'd earned it, but because I'm human and humans deserve kindness.

Why Self-Criticism Doesn't Work

Most of us believe that self-criticism is necessary for motivation. If we're too kind to ourselves, we'll become lazy, complacent, soft. We need the inner critic to keep us in line.

Research shows this is completely wrong.

When we criticize ourselves harshly, we activate our body's threat-defense system—the same fight-flight-freeze response that helps us deal with external danger. Our stress hormones spike. Our thinking narrows. We become defensive, avoidant, or paralyzed.

Self-criticism doesn't motivate; it immobilizes. It makes us less likely to try again after failure, less likely to take risks, less likely to pursue growth.

Self-compassion, on the other hand, activates our caregiving system. Our bodies release oxytocin and endorphins. We feel safe enough to acknowledge our mistakes without being destroyed by them. We can think clearly about what went wrong and what to do differently.

Self-criticism asks: What's wrong with you? Self-compassion asks: What do you need?

The second question is much more useful.

Building Resilience Through Self-Compassion

Resilience isn't something you're born with—it's built. It's built through facing challenges and discovering you can survive them, through falling down and getting back up, through learning that failure isn't the end of the story.

Self-compassion is the foundation of resilience. When you can treat yourself kindly after a setback, you're more likely to try again. When you can acknowledge pain without drowning in it, you recover faster. When you can see your struggles as part of the shared human experience rather than evidence of your personal inadequacy, you feel less alone.

Every time you face a hard thing and make it through, you're building resilience. Every time you fall and get back up, you're proving to yourself that you can handle hard things. Every time the critical voice says "you can't" and you move first, you're rewiring your brain to believe something different.

Resilience isn't about never struggling. It's about having the tools, the support, and the self-belief to recover from struggle. And those things can be developed at any age, after any amount of trauma, no matter how late you feel you're starting.

Part 3: Practicing Self-Compassion

Self-compassion isn't something you decide to have one day; it's something you practice until it becomes more natural. Like any skill, it takes repetition. Like any new habit, it feels awkward at first.

Start by noticing your self-talk. When you make a mistake, what do you say to yourself? Most of us wouldn't talk to a friend the way we talk to ourselves. We wouldn't call a struggling friend stupid or worthless or hopeless. But we say those things to ourselves all the time.

Try this: The next time you're struggling, place your hand on your heart. Take a breath. And say to yourself: "This is hard. Everyone struggles sometimes. May I be kind to myself in this moment."

It might feel awkward. It might feel fake. Move first. The feeling catches up.

Reflection: Your Self-Compassion Practice

Notice your inner dialogue this week. When you make a mistake, when something goes wrong, when you're not at your best—what does the voice in your head say?

Now ask: Would you say this to someone you love? If not, what would you say to them instead?

What's one small act of self-compassion you could practice this week? Maybe it's the hand-on-heart exercise. Maybe it's the high-five in the mirror. Maybe it's just pausing before the self-criticism starts and asking: What do I need right now?

You deserve your own kindness. Even if you don't believe that yet—especially if you don't believe that yet—practice acting as if you do. Sometimes the belief follows the behavior.

Move first. The feeling catches up.

The Science Behind "Move First"

The Science of Self-Compassion and Resilience

For most of my life, I believed that being hard on myself would make me better. That self-criticism was motivation. That if I just beat myself up enough, I would finally change.

The research shows this is completely backwards.

Kristin Neff and the Research on Self-Compassion

Dr. Kristin Neff is a professor at the University of Texas at Austin and the pioneer of self-compassion research. Her work has fundamentally changed how psychologists understand the relationship between how we treat ourselves and how well we function.

Neff defines self-compassion as treating yourself with the same kindness you would offer a good friend who was struggling. It sounds simple, but for most of us, it's revolutionary. We say things to ourselves that we would never say to someone we cared about. We hold ourselves to standards we would never impose on others. We beat ourselves up in ways we would recognize as abusive if directed at anyone else.

Self-compassion has three core components:

Self-kindness versus self-judgment: Treating yourself with warmth and understanding when you suffer, fail, or feel inadequate—rather than attacking yourself with criticism. This doesn't mean letting yourself off the hook; it means responding to your struggles with care rather than contempt.

Common humanity versus isolation: Recognizing that suffering and personal inadequacy are part of the shared human experience—not something that happens to "me" alone. Everyone struggles. Everyone fails. Everyone feels inadequate sometimes. You're not uniquely flawed; you're human.

Mindfulness versus over-identification: Holding your pain in balanced awareness rather than either suppressing it or being swept away by it. You acknowledge what you're feeling without letting it define you or consume you.

Here's what the research shows: self-compassion is not self-indulgence. It's not letting yourself off the hook. It's not weakness.

In fact, self-compassionate people are more motivated, not less. They have higher standards, not lower. They're more likely to take personal responsibility for mistakes—because they're not terrified of what acknowledging failure means about their worth. They can look clearly at their shortcomings because looking won't destroy them.

Self-compassion is also strongly linked to resilience. When self-compassionate people fail, they recover faster. They're less likely to spiral into depression or anxiety. They bounce back.

Why? Because self-criticism activates the threat-defense system—fight, flight, or freeze. When you attack yourself, your body responds as if it's under threat. Cortisol floods your system. Your heart rate increases. You go into survival mode. And survival mode is terrible for learning, growth, creativity, or positive change.

Self-compassion activates a different system entirely—the caregiving system. When you treat yourself with kindness, your body relaxes. Oxytocin is released. Your heart rate decreases. You feel safe enough to learn, grow, and change.

You can't hate yourself into change. But you can love yourself into it.

This doesn't mean you ignore your flaws or stop trying to improve. Self-compassion is the stable foundation from which improvement becomes possible. It's easier to acknowledge "I did something wrong" when you're not terrified it means "I am fundamentally bad." It's easier to try new things when failure doesn't mean annihilation.

Kelly McGonigal and the Stress Paradox

Dr. Kelly McGonigal is a health psychologist at Stanford University whose TED talk on stress has been viewed over 30 million times. Her research reveals something that seems impossible at first: your beliefs about stress can be more important than the stress itself.

In 1998, researchers asked 30,000 adults in the United States: "How much stress have you experienced in the last year?" They also asked: "Do you believe stress is harmful to your health?"

Then they tracked who died over the next eight years.

High levels of stress increased the risk of dying by 43%. That wasn't surprising. But here's the shocking finding: that increased risk only applied to people who believed stress was harmful to their health.

People who experienced high stress but didn't view it as harmful had no increased risk of dying. In fact, they had the lowest risk of dying of anyone in the study—even lower than people who reported relatively little stress.

The belief about stress mattered more than the stress itself.

McGonigal dug deeper into this finding and discovered that when we view stress as helpful—as the body mobilizing resources to meet a challenge—our physiological response actually changes. Our blood vessels stay relaxed instead of constricting (which is what makes chronic stress bad for the heart). Our heart responds more like it does during moments of joy and courage. We release more oxytocin, which strengthens social bonds and helps the heart recover from stress.

Same stressor. Different belief. Different physiological response. Different outcome.

This doesn't mean stress is good or that you should seek out more of it. But it does mean that your relationship to stress—how you think about it—is crucial.

McGonigal suggests a reframe: "My heart is pounding because my heart is in it. My body is responding because I care. This is my body preparing me to meet this challenge."

Instead of: "I'm so stressed, this is terrible for me."

This reframe transformed how I approach difficult moments. When I feel my heart racing before a challenge, I don't interpret it as evidence that I can't cope. I interpret it as evidence that I'm engaged, that I care, that my body is preparing to rise to the occasion.

The stress didn't change. My relationship to it did. And that changed everything.

Marsha Linehan and Opposite Action

Dr. Marsha Linehan is a professor at the University of Washington and the developer of Dialectical Behavior Therapy (DBT)—one of the most effective treatments for borderline personality disorder, suicidal behavior, and emotional dysregulation.

What many people don't know is that Linehan developed DBT partly from her own experience. As a young woman, she was hospitalized for severe mental illness, self-harmed, and was considered one of the most disturbed patients her doctors had seen. Later, after years of struggling and eventually finding her way to stability, she went on to become one of the most important psychologists of her generation.

From her personal experience and her clinical research, Linehan developed a skill called "Opposite Action"—one of the most powerful tools for changing emotions.

The principle is simple: every emotion creates an urge.

Fear creates the urge to avoid or run away. Sadness creates the urge to withdraw and isolate. Shame creates the urge to hide. Anger creates the urge to attack or lash out. Guilt creates the urge to repair or make amends.

These urges made sense in our evolutionary past. But in modern life, following them often makes things worse. Avoiding what we fear strengthens the fear. Withdrawing when we're sad deepens the depression. Hiding when we're ashamed reinforces the shame.

Opposite Action means doing the opposite of what the emotion urges—not to suppress the emotion, but to change it.

If fear tells you to avoid, you approach (gently, gradually). If sadness tells you to withdraw, you reach out and engage. If shame tells you to hide, you let yourself be seen. If anger tells you to attack, you step back and take space. If guilt tells you to avoid the person you've wronged, you make amends.

Research shows that Opposite Action reduces emotional distress faster than simply waiting for the feeling to pass or trying to think differently about the situation. Acting against the emotion's urge actually changes the emotion itself.

This is the behavioral foundation of "move first. The feeling catches up."

When I don't feel like getting out of bed, I get out of bed—and then I feel differently. When I don't feel like exercising, I exercise—and then I feel differently. When I don't feel like connecting with people, I reach out—and then I feel differently.

The action creates the emotional change. Not the other way around.

You don't have to feel different to act different. But acting different helps you feel different.

Putting It Into Practice: Building Resilience

How do you actually apply these findings to build self-compassion and resilience?

Treat yourself like you would a good friend. When you're struggling, ask: "What would I say to a friend in this situation?" Then say that to yourself.

Remember common humanity. You're not uniquely flawed. Whatever you're experiencing, millions of others have experienced it too. You're human, and humans struggle. This isn't isolation—it's connection.

Reframe stress. When you feel your stress response activate, try: "This is my body preparing me to meet this challenge. This response is helping me." The same physical sensations can be debilitating or empowering, depending on how you interpret them.

Practice Opposite Action. When your emotions urge you in a direction that will make things worse, try doing the opposite. Approach instead of avoid. Connect instead of withdraw. Let yourself be seen instead of hiding.

Cultivate mindful awareness. Notice your feelings without being swept away by them. "I'm feeling anxious" is different from "I am anxious." You can observe emotions without becoming them.

Remember: you can't hate yourself into change. Self-compassion isn't weakness—it's the foundation that makes sustainable change possible.

Reflection Questions

How do you typically talk to yourself when you make a mistake or face a setback? How would you talk to a good friend in the same situation?

Where might you be experiencing stress that could be reframed as your body preparing to meet a challenge?

What emotions are currently urging you in directions that might be making things worse? What would Opposite Action look like?

How do you relate to common humanity—the recognition that struggle and imperfection are universal human experiences?

What would it feel like to be truly compassionate toward yourself?

CHAPTER 7
PURPOSE
Move First... Even When You're Exhausted and Burned Out

Part 1: My Story

I spent over a decade working with the most challenging kids in the school system. The ones other teachers couldn't handle. The youngest kids, where early support could mean the difference between staying and being pushed out. The ones with trauma written all over their behavior—even if no one else could read it.

I got it. I understood them in a way that came from lived experience, not just training. When a kid was acting out—throwing desks, screaming, shutting down completely—I didn't see a problem child. I saw a wounded child using the only tools they had to survive. I saw myself.

I relied on behavior-based strategies—tools designed to help young kids succeed before discipline ever entered the picture. I could look at a behavior and see the function behind it. Every behavior serves a purpose, even the destructive ones. Kids don't act out because they're bad; they act out because they're trying to get something they need or avoid something that feels threatening. Once you understand the why, you can address the real problem instead of just punishing the symptom.

I spent fifteen years doing this work. Fifteen years of crisis de-escalation. Fifteen years of sitting with kids in their worst moments. I was trained in Therapeutic Crisis Intervention, in trauma-informed care, in the frameworks designed to help kids who'd been through more than they should have.

Somewhere along the way, helping these kids became my calling. Not just a job—a purpose.

But purpose has a cost when it's carried alone.

What changed me wasn't one child. It was all of them. Years of carrying other people's trauma inside my body. Years of walking into classrooms and crisis rooms, already braced for impact. Years of being the calm one while everything else was on fire. I learned how to regulate myself so others could regulate too. At first, that ability felt like a gift. It felt like this was exactly what I was meant to do.

But weight accumulates, even when you're strong.

Over time, the work began to take more than it gave. I watched the same patterns repeat—kids needing early support and getting it too late, families drowning while waiting for help, educators stretched beyond their limits and still expected to give more. I could see the solutions clearly, but I kept running into the same walls: policies, underfunding, impossible caseloads, systems built to manage behavior instead of heal it.

I was still helping. Still making a difference in the moments that mattered. But something inside me was eroding.

I wasn't just tired. I was burned out in a deeper way. The kind of exhaustion that comes from knowing the right thing to do and being unable to do it—not because you don't care or don't know how, but because the system won't allow it. Carrying that contradiction day after day takes a toll.

I felt it in my body. In my patience. In how thin my emotional reserves had become. I was showing up, but I was running on fumes. And beneath the exhaustion, a quiet truth kept surfacing: this wasn't sustainable.

Then my father died.

He struggled with addiction his entire life. He never got help. Never broke his own cycles. Watching him decline—watching him choose substances over his health, over his relationships, over life itself—was excruciating. And when he finally died, I felt something unexpected: relief.

Relief that he wasn't suffering anymore. Relief that I didn't have to watch him destroy himself. And alongside that relief came clarity.

I would do the work he never did.
I would break the cycles he couldn't break.
I would become someone who helps others do what he never figured out how to do.

That clarity made one thing undeniable: I couldn't keep doing this work in a way that was breaking me.

So I resigned from my job. Not because I didn't care— but because the circumstances no longer aligned with who I was becoming. The system was burning me out. I was constantly putting out fires instead of preventing them.

I felt nervous, uneasy, empowered, and hopeful all at once. That's what real transformation feels like—not confidence, but courage mixed with fear.

Now I'm in grad school, pursuing my master's. And in every class, I find myself thinking the same thing: I've lived this. I know this. My experience isn't just personal history—it's professional preparation.

I want to be the person I needed as a child. The adult who sees the wounded kid behind the behavior. The professional who understands that trauma isn't an excuse—it's an explanation. And explanations lead to solutions.

That's my purpose.
That's what I'm building toward.
And for the first time in my life, I can see it clearly.

Losing My Father

My father's death is a story that spans two years.

Two years of watching him decline. Two years of hospital visits and ultimatums and impossible choices. Two years of being one who showed up, carrying a weight that should have been shared but never was.

It started on Father's Day.

By then, I'd already pulled back from him. The drinking had become too much—not just the drinking itself, but everything that came with it. The chaos, the unpredictability, the feeling of being dragged into a crisis every time I got close. I was trying to build a healthy life, and his addiction kept threatening to pull me under.

But the messages wouldn't stop. Texts from family members, calls from people who knew him, everyone telling me the same thing: Your father is doing horrible. He's not taking care of himself. He's drinking himself to death.

And underneath the updates, always the accusation— spoken or implied: You need to fix this. You're his daughter. Don't abandon him at his worst. He needs family most right now.

The weight of that expectation was crushing. As if I could fix decades of addiction with enough love, enough presence, enough sacrifice. As if his choices were somehow my responsibility to undo. As if the only acceptable response to his self-destruction was to let it destroy me too.

But it was Father's Day. And despite everything—despite the boundaries I was trying to maintain, despite knowing it would cost me—I went to see him. Because that's what you do on Father's Day. Because some part of me still hoped that this time would be different. Because he was my father, and I loved him, and love makes us do things that logic can't explain.

The Chair

When I got to his house, I found him in his chair, withdrawing.

If you've never seen someone in alcohol withdrawal, you can't imagine how violent it is. The shakes weren't tremors— they were convulsions. His whole body was rebelling against itself, desperate for the poison it had become dependent on.

He was shaking so hard he couldn't stand, couldn't speak clearly, couldn't do anything but sit in that chair and vibrate with the force of his body's need.

I called my sister first. Get to his house, now. Something is really wrong.

Then I called an ambulance.

At the hospital, they discovered the burn blisters on his knees—he'd fallen asleep, drunk, outside in the sun and burned badly enough to blister. He was so far gone he hadn't even noticed, hadn't felt the pain, hadn't moved to protect himself from the damage being done to his own body.

He was in the hospital for six weeks. Four of those weeks were in the ICU, his body fighting to survive what he'd done to it. I visited. I sat with him. I watched machines breathe for him and monitors track his failing systems and nurses work to save a man who didn't seem interested in saving himself.

And then he got better. Against the odds, his body pulled through. He was released. He went home.

The first thing he did was grab a beer.

I lost it.

Six weeks of terror. Six weeks of watching him nearly die. Six weeks of hoping that maybe this would be the wake-up call, the rock bottom, the moment everything changed.

And he walked out of the hospital and reached for the very thing that had put him there.

The Long Decline

The next year and a half was a slow-motion nightmare.

The drinking continued. Then came the pills—painkillers, sedatives, anything that would numb him further. He was in and out of the hospital so many times I lost count. Each admission felt like a crisis; each discharge felt like a countdown to the next one.

I was there through almost of it. The one who showed up consistently. The one who sat in waiting rooms and talked to doctors and tried to coordinate care for someone who didn't want to be cared for.

Where was everyone else who had texted me about not abandoning him? When it came time to actually be present, to do the hard work of showing up day after day, they were nowhere to be found.

It's easy to tell someone else to save a drowning person. It's harder to jump in the water yourself.

Finally, after one of his hospital stays, I gave him an ultimatum. It was the hardest thing I'd ever said to him, and also the clearest:

"Go to rehab, or I will not be a part of your life anymore."

He agreed. He said yes, he would go, he was ready to change. For a moment—a brief, shining moment—I let myself hope.

Then the day came to actually go to rehab.

And he said no.

Just like that. No explanation, no negotiation, just a flat refusal to follow through on the promise he'd made. He would rather lose his daughter than give up the addiction.

I left the hospital that day. It was the last real conversation we ever had.

The Year of Silence

For almost a year, we didn't speak.

People judged me for it. How could you abandon your father? He's sick. He needs you. You only get one dad.

What they didn't understand—what you can't understand unless you've lived it—is that sometimes walking away is the only form of self-preservation available. I couldn't save him. I had tried everything, given everything, and it wasn't enough.

The only choice left was whether to drown alongside him or swim for shore.

I chose to swim.

During that year of silence, I did something that sounds cold but was actually necessary: I prepared myself for his death.

I knew it was coming. You don't drink and use pills the way he did and survive. His body had already nearly given out once; it was only a matter of time before it gave out for good. So I grieved him while he was still alive. I mourned the father I'd wished I had, the relationship we'd never have, the future we'd never share.

I let him go before he was gone.

It sounds harsh. Maybe it was. But it was also how I survived what came next.

The End

Almost exactly a year after our last conversation, I got the call.

My father was in the hospital again. Cardiac arrest. Brain dead. Seizing uncontrollably.

By the time I got there, there was nothing left to do but make a decision. His body was still going through the motions of life, but he was already gone. The machines could keep his heart beating indefinitely, but they couldn't bring back the person who used to live inside that failing body.

I had to make the call to take him off life support.

Me. The daughter who had "abandoned" him. The one everyone judged for walking away. When it came time to make the hardest decision of all, I was the one standing there holding my sister's hand. I was the one who had to say yes, let him go.

I was alone with my sister. Although I had been alone through all of it—the hospital visits, the ultimatums, the impossible choices. My sister and I were alone at the end, with our husbands at our sides.

I said goodbye to my father. I told him I loved him. I told him I forgave him—for the bars, for the chaos, for the ways he'd failed me and the ways I'd failed him. I told him it was okay to go.

And then I let him go.

Peace

Here's the truth I don't say out loud very often: his death didn't devastate me the way people expected it to.

I had already grieved. I had already prepared. I had already done the hard work of accepting that he was going to die and that I couldn't stop it. By the time death actually came, I had made my peace with it.

If we had still been close, if we had still been talking, if I hadn't had that year to process and prepare—it would have shattered me. But the distance I'd created, the boundary I'd drawn, the space I'd made between his chaos and my life—it protected me.

What I felt most, standing in that hospital room after they turned off the machines, was relief.

Relief that he wasn't suffering anymore. Relief that the long decline was finally over. Relief that he was free from the addiction that had imprisoned him his whole life.

My father was sick. He was depressed. His body hurt and his mind was trapped and he couldn't find his way out of the darkness he'd lived in for so long. He was determined, in some fundamental way, not to live. The drinking wasn't just a habit—it was a slow form of suicide, and I don't think he wanted to stop.

I couldn't save him. No one could. He didn't want to be saved.

I love my father. I always will. He was complicated and flawed and sometimes cruel, but he was also the man who rescued me from that dark house when I was four. He was the man who let me move back in at seventeen when I had nowhere else to go. He loved me the best way he knew how, even when his best wasn't nearly enough.

And now he's at peace. Finally, fully at peace.

That's not a tragedy. That's a mercy.

Rest now, Dad. You fought your demons for so long. You don't have to fight anymore.

Part 2: Aligning Values with Actions

What the Research Says About Purpose

Research on meaning and purpose consistently shows that people who feel their lives have meaning report higher life satisfaction, better physical health, and greater resilience in the face of challenges. Purpose isn't just nice to have—it's protective. It buffers against depression, helps people recover from setbacks, and provides a framework for making difficult decisions.

But here's what's important: purpose doesn't have to be grand. It doesn't have to be about saving the world or achieving greatness. Research shows that purpose can come from raising children well, from doing work that helps others, from creating things that bring beauty into the world, from simply being a good friend or neighbor.

What matters isn't the size of your purpose—it's the alignment between what you value and how you spend your time.

Values Clarification

Living with purpose requires knowing what you actually value—not what you think you should value, or what your family values, or what society tells you to value, but what genuinely matters to you.

For years, I didn't know. I was so busy surviving that I never stopped to ask what I wanted my life to be about. When you're in crisis mode, values feel like a luxury. You're just trying to make it through the day.

But as I healed, as the crisis became less constant, I had space to ask bigger questions. What do I actually care about? What kind of person do I want to be? What would make my life feel meaningful?

My answers: helping traumatized kids, breaking intergenerational cycles, being present for my family, continuing to grow and learn. Those values now guide my decisions. When something aligns with them, I move toward it. When something conflicts with them, I reconsider.

Purpose from Pain

Sometimes purpose finds you through pain. The thing you suffered through becomes the thing you're uniquely equipped to help others survive. That's not romanticizing trauma—that's transforming it. Taking what was meant to destroy you and using it to build something meaningful.

My childhood trauma prepared me to understand traumatized children in ways no textbook could. My addiction prepared me to have compassion for people struggling with substances. My years of feeling worthless prepared me to help others recognize their inherent value.

This doesn't mean trauma was good or necessary. It means I get to choose what to do with it now. I get to decide whether it defines me as a victim or equips me as a healer.

You get to make that choice too.

Part 3: Finding Your Path

Living with purpose doesn't mean everything is figured out. It means having a direction, even when the path is unclear. It means making choices that align with who you want to become, not just who you've been.

If you don't know your purpose yet, that's okay. Sometimes it reveals itself slowly, through experimentation and exploration. Try things. Notice what energizes you and what drains you. Pay attention to what makes you lose track of time, what makes you feel most like yourself.

And don't wait until you have it all figured out to start moving. Movement creates clarity. Action generates insight. You don't think your way to purpose—you act your way there.

Reflection: Your Purpose Exploration

Spend some time with these questions:

What experiences in your life—especially the hard ones—have given you unique insight or abilities? How might those experiences serve others?

What do you genuinely value? Not what you think you should value, but what actually matters to you?

What would it look like to move toward work or activities that align with your deepest values?

You don't need all the answers. You just need to start asking the questions.

The Science Behind "Move First"

The Science of Purpose and Mastery

Purpose isn't something you find by thinking about it. It's something you build through action—through showing up, through developing mastery, through contributing something meaningful.

Albert Bandura and Purpose

We discussed Bandura's self-efficacy research in Chapter 2. Here's what it means for purpose: the process of building mastery is itself meaningful.

When you work to develop competence—the sense of getting better, of overcoming challenges—you're engaged in one of the most satisfying human activities. Work that stretches us is more satisfying than work that's easy.

For fifteen years, I built mastery with challenging kids. Every crisis I managed added to my sense of competence. That competence gave my work meaning.

You don't find purpose by thinking. You build it by doing.

Amy Cuddy: Fake It Till You Become It

Dr. Amy Cuddy was a professor at Harvard Business School when she delivered one of the most-watched TED talks in history—over 70 million views and counting. Her research on "power poses" and presence has sparked both enthusiasm and controversy, but her core message remains valuable.

Cuddy's research showed that standing in confident postures—taking up space, expanding your body—for just two minutes could change how you feel. Specifically, it could increase feelings of power and decrease cortisol (the stress hormone).

But the research findings themselves are less important than the concept Cuddy introduced: "Fake it till you become it."

This is different from "fake it till you make it," which suggests pretending until you achieve some external outcome. "Fake it till you become it" is about acting in alignment with who you want to be until that identity becomes genuine.

This isn't about being inauthentic. It's about using behavior to shape identity. It's about recognizing that the person you're "pretending" to be might actually be you—a version of you that just hasn't fully emerged yet.

Cuddy developed this concept partly from her own experience. As a young woman, she survived a traumatic brain injury that significantly lowered her IQ. She was told she would never complete college, let alone achieve academic success. But she kept going—kept showing up, kept acting like someone who belonged in academia, even when she felt like a fraud.

Eventually, she realized she wasn't pretending anymore. She had become the thing she was acting like. The behavior had created the identity.

When I stood in front of classrooms full of struggling kids, I didn't always feel confident. I felt like I was making it up, pretending to be an authority I didn't feel. But I acted confident—I stood tall, spoke clearly, projected competence. And over time, the acting became real. I wasn't pretending anymore. I was the professional I had been rehearsing.

This is the "move first" of identity. You act like the person you want to become, even when it feels fake. And eventually, through repeated action, you actually become that person.

Cuddy writes: "Our bodies change our minds, and our minds change our behavior, and our behavior changes our outcomes."

Flow and the Psychology of Optimal Experience

Dr. Mihaly Csikszentmihalyi (pronounced "cheeks-sent-mee-HAY-ee") spent his career studying what he called "flow"—states of optimal experience where people are so absorbed in what they're doing that they lose track of time and feel intensely alive.

Flow happens when you're engaged in an activity that matches your skills to the challenge at hand. Too easy, and you're bored. Too hard, and you're anxious. But when the difficulty is just right—stretching you without overwhelming you—you enter flow.

In flow states, people report:

Complete absorption in the activity Loss of self-consciousness Distorted sense of time (usually time seems to pass quickly) Intrinsic enjoyment (the activity is its own reward) A sense of personal control and agency Clear goals and immediate feedback

Csikszentmihalyi found that flow is one of the primary sources of meaning and satisfaction in human life. People who experience more flow are happier, more productive, and more fulfilled.

The relevance to purpose is clear: flow happens when you're actively engaged in meaningful challenge. You can't flow your way through passivity. You have to be doing something—and doing something that stretches you.

This is another reason why "move first" matters. You don't wait to feel engaged to start an activity. You start the activity, and engagement often follows. You don't wait to feel flow to work on something challenging. You work on something challenging, and flow often emerges.

Purpose isn't a thing you find and then feel passionate about forever after. Purpose is something you build through repeated engagement with meaningful activities. Through mastery. Through flow. Through showing up and doing the work, even when you don't feel like it.

Putting It Into Practice: Building Purpose

How do you actually build purpose through action?

Seek mastery experiences. What could you work to become better at? The process of building competence is itself meaningful. Choose something that matters to you and commit to getting better at it.

Act like the person you want to become. What would that person do? How would they carry themselves? How would they spend their time? Start doing those things, even if it feels like pretending.

Find your flow activities. What activities absorb you? What makes you lose track of time? Seek out more of these activities—they're signposts pointing toward purpose.

Show up and do the work. Purpose clarifies through action, not contemplation. You don't think your way to your calling—you do your way there.

Remember: you don't find purpose by thinking. You build purpose by doing.

Reflection Questions

What activities bring you into flow states? How could you build more of these into your life?

What mastery are you currently building? What would you like to become better at?

If you were "acting like" the person you want to become, what would you be doing differently?

How has showing up—even when you didn't feel like it—revealed aspects of your purpose?

What work or contribution feels most meaningful to you? How did you discover this meaning?

CHAPTER 8
THE CYCLE BREAKER
Move First... Even When Terrified of Repeating the Past

Thomas: The Cycle Breaker

I need to tell you about my son.

Thomas is nineteen years old now. He'll always be my baby—that's just how it works when you've raised someone from infancy—but he's grown into this incredible young man that I can't quite believe came from me.

He was always an independent, easy-going kid. From the very beginning, he just had this calm energy, this quiet wisdom that seemed beyond his years. I joke with him sometimes: "I didn't have more kids because you were so great—I was afraid the next one would be a terror."

But here's the truth I have to tell you, the honest truth that I think matters more than any polished version of this story:

Thomas's childhood wasn't perfect. It wasn't magical. It wasn't untraumatic.

I wasn't the mother I wish I had been. During his formative years, I was struggling with addiction, with my own unprocessed trauma, with trying to survive each day. I was emotionally dysregulated. Short-tempered. Easily frustrated. My nervous system had been offline and broken my whole life, and I didn't have the tools to regulate myself, let alone model regulation for my child.

I look back at those years and cringe. The times I yelled when I should have stayed calm. The times I was too overwhelmed to be fully present. The times my own trauma spilled over onto him in ways I couldn't control.

Thomas was quiet. Withdrawn. And I've wondered, more times than I can count: Was that just his personality? Or was that a survival strategy—a child learning to stay small and invisible because his mother was too overwhelmed to handle anything more?

I'll never know for sure. And that uncertainty haunts me.

But here's what I do know: despite everything, despite my failures and shortcomings, we gave Thomas a loving home. Two parents who cared about him deeply, who stayed together, who worked through their issues instead of abandoning each other or him. His life wasn't perfect—whose is?—but love was the constant. Love was the foundation. Even when I couldn't give him the regulated, calm mother he deserved, I could give him love.

And apparently, that was enough.

The Moment I Knew

The other day, Thomas told me something that stopped me in my tracks.

He said he doesn't hang out with his friends much anymore. When I asked why, he said, "They do things I don't want to do."

Let that sink in for a moment.

At nineteen years old, my son is choosing to distance himself from peer pressure. He's choosing his values over fitting in. He's choosing not to go down the path that destroyed his "grandmother," his grandfather, and nearly destroyed his mother.

I looked at him and said, "Thomas, do you realize what you're doing? You're breaking generational trauma. You're breaking the addiction cycle. That's amazing."

He kind of shrugged, the way nineteen-year-olds do when their moms get emotional. But I could tell it landed. He heard me.

He's seen what addiction does. Up close and personal. He watched his grandfather—his best friend for so much of his childhood—deteriorate and die from it. He watched me struggle and claw my way back to sobriety. He's been told, again and again, about the patterns in our family, the genetic predisposition, the importance of making good choices.

Every time he leaves the house, I say the same thing: "I love you. Have fun. Be safe. Make good choices."

Every single time. Without fail. For years.

Maybe he got tired of hearing it. Maybe it became background noise. Or maybe—just maybe—it sank in. Maybe hearing those words over and over planted something that's now bearing fruit.

What Breaking the Cycle Really Looks Like

Here's what I've learned about intergenerational trauma: you don't break it 100%. You break it enough.

I couldn't give Thomas what I never received. I couldn't model emotional regulation I was never taught. I couldn't provide the calm, stable environment that I never experienced. I couldn't be perfect, because I was learning how to be functional at the same time I was trying to raise him.

But I could love him fiercely. I could stay. I could try. I could keep showing up, even when I was failing, even when I was struggling, even when I wanted to give up.

And I could give him something my parents never gave me: awareness.

I told Thomas the truth about our family. About addiction. About mental health. About the patterns that can trap you if you don't see them coming. I didn't hide our history or pretend we were normal or let him walk into adulthood blind to the risks he carries in his genes.

Thomas did inherit some of my dysregulation. He's short-tempered sometimes, easily frustrated. But here's the difference: he knows it. He's aware of it. He's actively working on it at nineteen years old, recognizing patterns in himself that I didn't recognize until I was thirty.

He's starting his healing journey a decade earlier than I did.

That's not failure on my part. That's progress. That's what realistic cycle-breaking looks like. Not perfection—improvement. Not zero trauma passed on—less trauma passed on. Not a complete fix—a better starting point.

What Thomas Taught Me

Here's something that wrecks me in the best way:

When I think about Thomas's childhood, I can only recall my mistakes. The times I yelled. The times I was too overwhelmed to be present. The times I let my trauma spill over onto him. Those memories play on repeat, a highlight reel of my failures as a mother.

But when Thomas talks about his childhood? He tells me all the good stuff.

He remembers the love. He remembers that we cared. He remembers feeling safe, even when things were chaotic, because he knew his parents loved him.

Maybe I'm harder on myself than I deserve. Maybe the moments I remember as catastrophic weren't as damaging as I fear. Or maybe Thomas is resilient in ways I don't fully understand. Either way, hearing him talk about his childhood with fondness rather than resentment is a gift I never expected to receive.

Thomas works full-time now. He's figuring out life, the way nineteen-year-olds do—trying things, making mistakes, learning as he goes. We have this parallel play thing in our house—we're often in separate rooms doing our own things, comfortable in our own spaces.

But when we do hang out, it's magical. We have the deepest conversations. He's wise beyond his years, and he's become one of my best friends. We grew up together, in a way—I was so young when I had him. We've both been figuring out life at the same time.

Thomas will be the first person to read this book before I publish it. Because this story is his story too. Because he lived through so much of it. Because he deserves to know what I'm sharing, to have a say, to tell me if anything feels wrong or too exposed.

And because his opinion matters more to me than any critic's ever could.

Everything I've been through, everything I've survived, everything I've worked so hard to overcome—it led me here. To this moment. To this book. To a life I never thought I'd have.

Because I raised a son who chooses good.

Because I raised a cycle breaker.

Because I raised Thomas.

Part 2: The Science of Cycle-Breaking

Research on intergenerational trauma transmission shows that cycles can be interrupted through several key factors: awareness of family patterns, access to alternative models of behavior, emotional support during development, and intentional effort to do things differently.

What I gave Thomas wasn't perfection—it was awareness and intention. I named the patterns. I explained the risks. I modeled recovery, even when that recovery was messy and imperfect. I showed him that change was possible, that cycles could be broken, that the past didn't have to dictate the future.

Studies also show that secure attachment in at least one relationship can buffer a child against the effects of trauma and dysfunction in other relationships. I couldn't protect Thomas from all the effects of my struggles. But I could make sure he knew, without question, that he was loved.

That love was the thread that held everything together. It wasn't enough to prevent all harm—nothing is. But it was enough to provide a foundation for healing.

Reflection: Your Triumph Moments

What are the moments in your life—big or small—when you triumphed? When you survived something you weren't sure you could? When you made a choice that broke an old pattern?

Write them down if you can. These are your proof that you can do hard things. These are the evidence that change is possible. These are your triumph moments, and they matter— not because they're impressive to anyone else, but because they're yours.

You made it through. You're still here. That matters more than you might realize.

The Science Behind "Move First"

The Science of Breaking Cycles

Thomas is breaking generational cycles. This isn't just a nice metaphor—it's something the research shows is genuinely possible, though not easy. Understanding the science of intergenerational trauma and its interruption can help us appreciate what Thomas is doing and what any of us can do.

Intergenerational Trauma and Epigenetics

For most of history, trauma was considered an individual experience. What happened to you affected you. End of story.

We now know this is incomplete.

Research on intergenerational trauma has shown that the effects of traumatic experiences can be passed from one generation to the next. Children of Holocaust survivors show elevated rates of PTSD. Grandchildren of those who experienced severe famine show metabolic differences. The trauma of one generation echoes in subsequent generations.

How does this happen? Through multiple pathways:

Behavioral transmission: Traumatized parents may parent differently—more anxiously, more punitively, less warmly. Their children learn patterns of relating and coping that reflect the parents' trauma, even if the children didn't directly experience the traumatic events.

Social transmission: Families develop narratives, beliefs, and ways of being that are shaped by trauma. These get passed down as "the way things are" or "what our family is like."

Biological transmission: This is where the science gets really interesting. Epigenetics—the study of how gene expression can change without changes to the DNA sequence itself—has shown that traumatic experiences can literally change which genes are turned on or off. And some of these epigenetic changes can be inherited.

Studies of mice have shown that a fear response can be passed to offspring who never experienced the original trauma. Studies of humans have shown epigenetic changes in children of trauma survivors. We carry our ancestors' experiences in our very cells.

This might sound depressing. If trauma is literally written into our biology, how can we escape it?

But here's the hopeful part: epigenetic changes are reversible. Just as trauma can change gene expression, so can healing. Positive experiences can turn different genes on and off. Intervention can change the biological inheritance.

And behavioral and social transmission—the main ways trauma passes between generations—can absolutely be interrupted. They don't require changing your DNA. They require changing your behavior, your beliefs, your ways of relating.

This is what Thomas is doing. He's interrupting the behavioral and social transmission of family patterns. He's making different choices than the ones that were modeled for him. He's breaking the cycle—not perfectly, not completely, but enough.

What Research Shows About Breaking Cycles

Studies on breaking intergenerational cycles have identified several key factors:

Awareness of family patterns: Simply knowing that certain behaviors or struggles run in your family increases the likelihood of change. The pattern loses some of its power when it's named and understood.

Alternative models: Seeing people—ideally people you can identify with—who have made different choices provides a template for change. If you've never seen healthy relationships, it's hard to create one. But if you see even one example, possibilities open up.

At least one secure attachment: Having at least one relationship characterized by warmth, consistency, and emotional safety can buffer against the effects of dysfunction in other relationships. This is one of the most robust findings in developmental psychology.

Intentional effort: Breaking cycles requires conscious, deliberate action. The patterns were learned; they must be unlearned. This takes ongoing commitment.

Support and resources: Change is easier with help—therapy, support groups, mentors, books. The more resources you can access, the more likely you are to succeed.

What Thomas has:

He has awareness. I told him the truth about our family—about addiction, about trauma, about the patterns that can trap you. He knows what he's up against.

He has alternative models. He watched me transform. He's seen that change is possible, that patterns can be broken.

He has secure attachment. Whatever my failures as a mother, I gave him love. Consistent, unconditional, present love. He knew he was loved, even when I couldn't give him everything else he deserved.

He's making intentional effort. His choice to distance himself from friends who "do things I don't want to do" is intentional. He's consciously choosing different patterns.

And he started earlier than I did. He's making these choices at nineteen. I wasn't making them until thirty.

Neuroplasticity and New Pathways (Revisited)

Remember neuroplasticity—the brain's ability to change and form new neural connections throughout life? This is exactly what Thomas is demonstrating.

Every time he says no to choices that would continue family patterns, he's physically strengthening neural pathways for different behaviors. Every time he chooses awareness over avoidance, he's rewiring himself for a different future.

The patterns that took generations to establish can begin to shift in a single generation—not through perfection, but through awareness and intentional action.

This is the science of cycle-breaking: it's possible. Not guaranteed. Not easy. But possible. And each generation that tries makes it a little easier for the next.

The Power of "Good Enough"

Donald Winnicott, a British pediatrician and psychoanalyst, coined the term "good enough mother" (later expanded to "good enough parent"). His insight was that children don't need perfect parents—they need parents who are good enough.

Good enough means: responsive most of the time, though not always. Attuned, though not perfectly. Present and loving, though human and fallible.

Winnicott observed that parents who try to be perfect often do more harm than good. The child never learns that rupture can be repaired, that mistakes can be survived, that imperfection is survivable. But good enough parents model something crucial: they mess up, they repair, and life goes on. The child learns resilience.

This concept transformed how I think about my parenting. I wasn't perfect. I yelled when I should have stayed calm. I was overwhelmed when I should have been present. I let my trauma spill onto Thomas in ways I'll always regret.

But I was good enough. I was there. I loved him. I kept showing up. And when I messed up, I tried to repair.

Good enough broke the cycle. Not completely—Thomas inherited some of my dysregulation, some of my patterns. But he inherited less than I inherited from my parents. And he's starting his healing journey earlier than I started mine.

That's what cycle-breaking looks like. Not perfection—improvement. Not zero transmission—reduced transmission. Not complete fix—better starting point.

Putting It Into Practice: Breaking Your Cycles

How do you actually break intergenerational cycles?

Develop awareness. What patterns run in your family? What behaviors, beliefs, or struggles keep showing up across generations? Naming them is the first step to changing them.

Seek alternative models. Find people—in your life, in books, in media—who have broken similar cycles. You need to see that it's possible before you can believe it for yourself.

Invest in secure relationships. If you didn't have them growing up, seek them now—through therapy, through chosen family, through intentional relationships. It's never too late to experience secure attachment.

Make intentional choices. Breaking cycles isn't passive. It requires actively choosing different behaviors, different responses, different patterns—over and over again.

Aim for good enough, not perfect. You won't break the cycle completely. You'll pass some things on. The goal isn't perfection—it's improvement. Less damage. Better foundation. Easier starting point for the next generation.

Reflection Questions

What cycles have you witnessed in your family across generations? What patterns keep repeating?

How aware of these patterns were you before you started doing healing work? What difference has awareness made?

Who in your life has modeled breaking similar cycles? How has their example influenced you?

Where are you breaking cycles, even imperfectly? What differences are you creating?

If you have or plan to have children, what do you most want to give them that you didn't receive?

CHAPTER 9
MOMENTUM
Move First... Even When Motivation Disappears

Part 1: My Story

My alarm goes off at 4:45 AM every single day.

Not because I'm a morning person—I'm really not. But because I've learned that the morning hours, before the world wakes up and starts demanding things from me, are sacred. They're mine.

I wake up, I make my coffee, and I sit with myself before the day begins. Sometimes I meditate. Sometimes I journal. Sometimes I just stare out the window and let my thoughts settle. The dogs are usually still sleeping—Bruno stretched out on his bed, Otis and Lyla curled up in their crates—and the house is quiet in a way it never is during the day.

This morning routine didn't happen overnight. I built it slowly, one habit at a time, over years of trial and error. There were months when I couldn't get out of bed, when the depression was so heavy that 4:45 AM felt like a cruel joke. There were seasons when my routines fell apart completely, when survival took all my energy, and there was nothing left for self-care.

But I kept coming back. That's the secret, if there is one: not perfection, but persistence. Not getting it right every time, but getting back to it after you fall off.

People sometimes call me selfish for prioritizing my morning routine, my workouts, and my self-care. "Must be nice to have time for all that," they say, with an edge in their voice that suggests I'm doing something wrong by taking care of myself.

Here's what I've learned: I AM selfish. And I say that proudly now.

Not selfish in the way that hurts others. Selfish in the way that fills my cup so I have something to pour out. Selfish in the way that recognizes I can't help anyone else if I'm running on empty. Selfish in the way that, finally, after thirty-five years, treats myself like someone worth taking care of.

For most of my life, I put everyone else first. My son, my partner, my job, my family—everyone got pieces of me until there was nothing left. And then I wondered why I was exhausted, depressed, burnt out, reaching for a drink just to get through the day.

Now I understand: you can't give what you don't have. And you can't maintain momentum if you're constantly depleted.

The Reality of Partnership

I told you earlier that Jose and I don't have a perfect love story. I want to expand on that, because I think it's important.

After seventeen years together, I've learned something that took me a long time to understand: love isn't about shaping another person into who you think they should be. It's about accepting who they are, while continuing to grow into who *you* are becoming. Our relationship has taught me that partnership isn't about control, fixing, or keeping score—it's about choice.

For a long time, I believed that if I just showed up better, communicated better, loved harder, everything would fall neatly into place. I thought love was something you *did* to improve a relationship, rather than something you practiced *within* it. I had to learn that two people don't merge into one perfect unit just because they commit to each other. They remain two individuals, walking side by side.

Living a life with another human being is layered. It's beautiful and complicated and, at times, exhausting. There are moments of deep connection and moments of misunderstanding. There are days when you feel perfectly aligned and days when you feel worlds apart. That doesn't mean something is broken—it means something real is happening.

What changed everything for me was turning my attention inward. Focusing on my own growth. My own regulation. My own values. Not as a withdrawal from the relationship, but as a way to strengthen it. I learned that when I take responsibility for myself, I show up as a better partner.

And here's the part that matters most: we choose each other. Not once. Not just when it's easy. Every single day.

Jose sees me living intentionally—prioritizing my health, honoring my boundaries, and doing the work to be more grounded and present. I see him showing up in the ways he knows how. We notice each other. We respect each other's pace. We give each other room to be human.

What we have isn't a polished, picture-perfect partnership. It's something more meaningful. Two people who keep trying. Who keep choosing patience over pressure. Curiosity over judgment. Love over the need to be right.

I'm not here to fix him. He's not here to complete me. We walk alongside each other, supporting without forcing, loving without conditions, growing without deadlines.

That's what real partnership looks like after seventeen years. Not perfection. Not constant harmony. But commitment. Effort. And the quiet, powerful decision to keep choosing each other—exactly as we are, today and every day.

Part 2: The Science of Sustainable Change

Habits and Identity

Research on habit formation shows something crucial: the most lasting changes happen at the identity level, not the behavior level.

Here's what that means: Instead of saying "I'm trying to exercise more," you say "I'm someone who exercises." Instead of "I'm trying to quit drinking," you say "I'm someone who doesn't drink." The shift is subtle but powerful. You're not fighting against yourself to do something that feels unnatural. You're becoming someone for whom the behavior is natural.

For me, the identity shift happened gradually. I used to be someone who drank to cope. Now I'm someone who hikes, who does yoga, who walks her dogs at sunrise. I didn't just change my behaviors—I changed who I am.

This is why the work is ongoing. You don't just decide to be different one day and then you're done. You practice being the person you want to become, over and over, until that person becomes who you actually are.

The Power of Non-Negotiables

One of the most powerful concepts I've learned is the idea of non-negotiables—things you do no matter what, regardless of how you feel, regardless of what else is happening in your life.

My morning routine is non-negotiable. Moving my body is non-negotiable. Taking care of my dogs is non-negotiable. These aren't things I decide to do each day based on motivation or energy. They're just things I do. Period.

Non-negotiables remove decision fatigue. When something is truly non-negotiable, you don't have to spend mental energy deciding whether to do it today. You just do it. The decision has already been made, once and for all.

This is especially important for those of us with trauma histories, because our brains are already overwhelmed. Every decision we can remove from our daily mental load is a gift to ourselves.

Momentum Creates Momentum

Physics teaches us that objects in motion tend to stay in motion. The same is true for personal growth. The hardest part is starting. Once you have momentum, it becomes easier to maintain.

That's why small wins matter so much. Each small win builds evidence that change is possible. Each completed morning routine, each workout finished, each day sober—they add up. They create momentum. They make the next day easier.

But momentum can also work against you. Miss one day, and it's easier to miss the next. Skip your routine once, and the exception starts to become the rule. This is why getting back on track quickly matters so much. Not perfection—persistence.

Part 3: Building Your Momentum

Maintaining momentum isn't about doing everything right. It's about having systems that get you back on track when you fall off. It's about knowing your non-negotiables and protecting them. It's about building an identity around who you want to become, not just what you want to do.

Start small. One non-negotiable. One morning routine element. One thing you do no matter what. Build from there.

Reflection: Your Non-Negotiables

What's one thing you could make non-negotiable in your life? Something that supports your wellbeing, your growth, your becoming the person you want to be?

Start with just one. Make it small enough to be sustainable. And then protect it fiercely.

Remember: you can't pour from an empty cup. Taking care of yourself isn't selfish—it's necessary. And you are worth taking care of.

The Science Behind "Move First"

The Science of Maintaining Change

Transformation isn't a single moment—it's a daily practice. The research on maintaining behavior change shows us what actually sustains new patterns over time.

Identity-Based Habits (Deep Dive)

We touched on James Clear's concept of identity-based habits earlier. Now let's go deeper, because this is crucial for maintenance.

Clear argues that there are three levels at which change can occur:

Outcomes: What you get. Goals live here. Processes: What you do. Habits and systems live here. Identity: What you believe. Your sense of who you are lives here.

Most people try to change by starting with outcomes: I want to lose 20 pounds. I want to write a book. I want to be sober.

But outcome-based change is fragile. You're essentially trying to become a different person while still seeing yourself as the old person. It creates cognitive dissonance—you act one way but think of yourself another way. Eventually, identity wins and you snap back.

The alternative is to start with identity: I'm someone who takes care of their body. I'm a writer. I'm a person who doesn't drink.

When identity shifts first, behavior follows naturally. You don't have to force yourself to exercise when you genuinely see yourself as someone who exercises—that's just what you do. You don't have to struggle against drinking when you genuinely see yourself as someone who doesn't drink—that option isn't on the table.

Clear explains: "Every action you take is a vote for the type of person you wish to become. No single instance will transform your beliefs, but as the votes build up, so does the evidence of your new identity."

This is why consistency matters more than intensity for maintenance. Each time you show up—even minimally— you're casting another vote for your new identity. You're building evidence. You're reinforcing who you're becoming.

I'm no longer someone who drank to cope. That's not willpower—that's identity. Drinking doesn't fit with who I am now. The identity holds the behavior in place.

The Habit Loop and Maintenance

Charles Duhigg, in "The Power of Habit," describes the habit loop: cue → routine → reward.

A cue triggers the behavior. The routine is the behavior itself. The reward reinforces the behavior.

For maintenance, understanding this loop is crucial because you can't simply eliminate bad habits—you have to replace them. The cue isn't going away. The need for reward isn't going away. What you can change is the routine that happens in between.

This is what happened with my Saturday mornings. The cue (Saturday morning) used to trigger drinking. Now it triggers walking with Jose. The cue is the same. The need for reward (relaxation, pleasure, connection) is the same. But the routine has been replaced.

Duhigg calls this the "Golden Rule of Habit Change": keep the cue and reward, change the routine.

For maintaining change long-term, it helps to identify:

What are the cues that used to trigger your old behavior? What rewards were you seeking through that behavior? What new routines can deliver similar rewards in response to the same cues?

When you can answer these questions, maintenance becomes much more sustainable. You're not fighting the habit loop—you're working with it.

The Role of Environment

Dr. Anne Thorndike led a study at Massachusetts General Hospital that demonstrated something powerful about maintenance. By rearranging the hospital cafeteria to make healthy options more visible and accessible, she increased healthy food sales by 25%—without any education, persuasion, or appeals to willpower.

The research on environment and behavior change is consistent: your environment shapes your behavior more than you realize. If you want to maintain change, design your environment to make the desired behavior easier and the undesired behavior harder.

For maintenance, this means:

Remove friction from good behaviors. If you want to exercise in the morning, lay out your workout clothes the night before. If you want to eat healthy, keep healthy food visible and convenient.

Add friction to undesired behaviors. If you want to stop mindless phone-scrolling, put your phone in another room. If you want to stop drinking, don't keep alcohol in the house.

Surround yourself with people who embody the change you want. We become like the people we spend time with. If everyone around you drinks heavily, maintaining sobriety is hard. If your social circle supports and models healthy behavior, maintenance is easier.

I designed my mornings to make my routines inevitable. The coffee is set up the night before. My walking shoes are by the door. The dogs are eager to go out. Everything about my environment points me toward my morning routine. I don't have to decide each day—the environment decides for me.

Self-Monitoring and Feedback

Research consistently shows that self-monitoring—tracking your behavior—significantly improves both initial change and maintenance.

When people keep food diaries, they lose more weight. When people track their exercise, they exercise more. When people in recovery maintain daily check-ins, they stay sober longer.

Why does self-monitoring work?

It increases awareness. You can't change what you don't notice. It provides feedback. You can see patterns, progress, and problems. It creates accountability, even if just to yourself. It keeps the commitment present and active in your mind.

For maintenance, some form of regular check-in is valuable. This might be a journal, an app, a conversation with a trusted person, or simply a daily moment of reflection.

I'm not a rigorous tracker, but I do check in with myself. Each morning during my quiet time, I take stock. How am I doing? What needs attention? What went well yesterday? What do I want to be mindful of today? This regular self-monitoring helps me catch slippage before it becomes relapse.

The Importance of Non-Negotiables

BJ Fogg's research emphasizes the power of what he calls "non-negotiables"—behaviors you do no matter what, regardless of how you feel, with no exceptions.

For trauma survivors, this is especially important. Our brains are already overwhelmed with decisions and emotional management. Having non-negotiables removes decision fatigue. You don't decide whether to do the thing—you just do it.

My morning routine includes non-negotiables: I get up at 5:30. I do my quiet time. I walk the dogs. I move my body in some way.

These aren't goals I hope to achieve. They're identities I embody. They're non-negotiable.

The power of non-negotiables is that they survive bad days. When motivation is low, when emotions are overwhelming, when life is chaotic—the non-negotiables keep happening because they're not subject to debate.

Putting It Into Practice: Maintaining Your Change

Establish non-negotiables—behaviors you do no matter what. Design your environment to support them. Self-monitor regularly. And remember: consistency beats intensity.

Reflection Questions

What non-negotiables do you have (or want to have) in your life?

How could you redesign your environment to make your desired behaviors easier?

What cues trigger your old behaviors? What new routines could you substitute?

How do you currently monitor your progress? What form of check-in might help with maintenance?

Who you are becoming? How are your daily actions voting for that identity?

CHAPTER 10
FORWARD
Move First... Even When You Can't See the Whole Path

Part 1: My Story

I started this book by telling you I was abandoned at four years old. That I was pregnant at fifteen. That I spent years drowning in alcohol, substances, and trauma, and the belief that I was fundamentally broken.

I want to end by telling you where I am now.

I'm thirty-five years old. I'm in graduate school, and I wake up at 4:45 every morning to work on myself before I work on anything else. I have three pit bulls who keep me grounded, a son who makes me proud, and a partner who, despite our imperfections, has chosen me for seventeen years.

I'm writing this book—this book that you're holding—which is something the abandoned little girl in the dark house never could have imagined.

I'm not healed. I want to be clear about that. Healing isn't a destination you arrive at, and then you're done. It's an ongoing process, a daily practice, a commitment you make over and over again. Some days are harder than others. Some weeks I feel like I've figured it all out, and other weeks I feel like I'm right back at the beginning.

But I'm moving forward. That's what matters. Not perfection—progress. Not arrival—direction.

What I Want You to Remember

If you take nothing else from this book, I want you to remember these things:

Your trauma is real. It happened. It hurt. And acknowledging that isn't weakness—it's the first step toward healing. You don't have to minimize what you've been through or pretend it was fine. It wasn't fine. And you survived it anyway.

Your worth is inherent. You don't have to earn it. You can't lose it. It doesn't depend on what you do or don't do, what you achieve or fail at, who approves of you or doesn't. You are worthy because you exist. Full stop.

Change is possible. I know it doesn't always feel that way. I know there are days when you're convinced you'll never be different, that the patterns are too deep, that the damage is too extensive. But I'm living proof that transformation happens. Not overnight. Not easily. But it happens.

You can do hard things. You've already proven this. You've survived things that could have destroyed you. You're still here, still reading, still looking for a way forward. That's strength. That's resilience. That's proof that you have what it takes.

You don't have to do it alone. Find your people. Find your support. Find the friends, the therapists, the books, the podcasts, the communities that remind you of who you're becoming. You weren't meant to carry this alone.

Your Invitation

I don't know what brought you to this book. Maybe you're in crisis right now, looking for any reason to keep going. Maybe you're in recovery, looking for someone who understands. Maybe you're just curious, or a friend gave this to you, or you stumbled across it by accident.

Whatever brought you here, I'm glad you came.

And now I want to invite you into what comes next.

This isn't the end of your story. It's not even the end of mine. It's just a moment—a pause in the journey where I've shared what I've learned so far, and you've listened.

What happens next is up to you.

You can put this book down and go back to exactly how things were. That's a choice. I won't judge you for it. Sometimes we're not ready. Sometimes the timing isn't right. Sometimes survival takes all our energy, and there's nothing left for growth.

Or you can take one small step. Just one. Start with the morning. Start with a journal. Start with a conversation you've been avoiding. Start with finally calling a therapist. Start with putting down the drink, just for today.

You don't have to transform overnight. You just have to begin.

And if you've already begun—if you're already on this path, already doing the work, already fighting for a better life— then keep going. Don't stop now. The world needs you healed. Your family needs you healed. YOU DESERVE to be healed.

I believe in you. Even if we've never met. Even if I'll never know your name. I believe in your capacity to change, to grow, to become someone you're proud of.

Because I've seen it happen. I've lived it.

And if I can do it—the abandoned girl, the teenage mother, the woman who wanted to die—then so can you.

You are worthy.

You always have been.

Now go live like it.

THE END

(but really, just the beginning)

The Science Behind Move First

The Complete Science of Moving First

Throughout this book, I've woven together insights from some of the most influential psychological research of the past century. Now I want to bring it all together—the science behind why Move First works.

At its core, Move First is simple but radical:

you don't wait to feel ready. You act—and readiness follows.

This isn't just a mindset. It's a pattern supported by decades of research across psychology, neuroscience, and behavior change.

The Researchers and What They Reveal

William James showed us that action creates emotion. We don't act because we feel motivated; we often feel motivated because we act. You don't have to wait for the feeling—movement can create it.

Martin Seligman showed us that helplessness is learned—and that agency can be relearned. When you take action and see that your behavior matters, your brain updates its beliefs. Action restores agency.

Viktor Frankl showed us that meaning sustains us through suffering. But meaning isn't found through endless reflection—it's built through engagement with life. Through participation. Through action.

Angela Duckworth showed us that effort and persistence matter more than talent. Progress comes from continuing forward even when it's uncomfortable, imperfect, or slow.

Carol Dweck showed us that struggle isn't failure—it's the mechanism of growth. When challenges are framed as part of learning, action becomes safer and more sustainable.

BJ Fogg showed us that small actions, done consistently, create powerful change. You don't need a breakthrough moment. You need a starting point.

Kelly McGonigal showed us that our interpretation of stress shapes our outcomes. When stress is seen as preparation rather than danger, action becomes possible again.

Marsha Linehan showed us that behavior can lead emotion. Acting opposite to avoidance or fear can soften those emotions over time.

Kristin Neff showed us that self-compassion isn't indulgent—it's essential. Sustainable change requires support, not self-punishment.

Albert Bandura showed us that confidence isn't a prerequisite—it's built through mastery experiences. Each action becomes evidence of capability.

Amy Cuddy showed us that behavior shapes identity. Acting like the person you want to become helps that identity take root.

Walter Mischel showed us that effective self-control relies on strategy, not willpower.

Peter Gollwitzer showed us that specific action plans dramatically increase follow-through.

James Clear showed us that habits are votes for identity. Who you become is shaped by what you repeatedly do.

And neuroplasticity research shows us that every action physically changes the brain. What you practice strengthens. What you avoid weakens.

The Unified Message
Beneath all of this research is one clear truth:

You don't need to feel ready to act.
You act—and readiness follows.

This is the science of Move First.
Not motivation first. Not clarity first.
Movement first.

Old patterns tell you nothing you do will matter.
Action teaches your brain otherwise.

Old beliefs tell you you're not capable.
Action builds evidence that you are.

Fear tells you to stay small.
Action shows you what you can handle.

You are not stuck.
Your brain can change.
Your identity can shift.
Your patterns can be rewritten.

Not through thinking alone.
Through doing.

Your Invitation

I've shared my story.
I've shared the science.
Now it's your turn.

Not: What do you want to do someday?
Not: What will you do when you feel ready?
Not: What would you do if things were different?

What will you move on first—right now, as you are, with what you have?

The science says this works.
The research supports it.
The evidence is clear.

But no study can take the step for you.
No theory can make the choice.

You have to move first.
The feeling will catch up.

Final Reflection Questions:

Which ideas or studies from this book resonated most strongly with you? Which challenged you?

What is one action you've been waiting to feel ready for that you could take today?

What small "votes" could you cast today for the identity you want to build?

When old patterns pull you toward stillness, how will you remind yourself to move first?

What is your first move—the action that carries you forward even when comfort, fear, or doubt tells you not to?

THE MOVE FIRST MANIFESTO

Ten Truths:

1. When your past tells you you're broken, move first. You are not the worst thing that happened to you. You are the person who survived it. Your past wrote the old story. Your actions write the new one.

2. When you don't feel worthy, move first. Your worth is inherent. It doesn't depend on achievements or anyone's opinion. Act anyway. Let the doing build the believing.

3. When fear tells you to stay small, move first. Fear is information, not instruction. You don't have to stop being afraid to take action. You take action afraid, and the fear loosens its grip.

4. When failure seems certain, move first. Failure isn't the opposite of success—it's part of the path. Every attempt teaches you something. The only true failure is never trying.

5. When people doubt you, move first. Their doubt is about their limitations, not yours. You don't need anyone's permission to become who you're meant to be.

6. When the path seems impossible, move first. You don't need to see the whole staircase—just the next step. The impossible becomes possible one tiny action at a time.

7. When you want to give up, move first. The moment you want to quit is often right before breakthrough. Rest if you need to—rest is not quitting. But don't stop.

8. When you feel alone, move first. You are not as alone as you feel. Reach out. Connect. Let yourself be seen. You are part of a vast invisible community of survivors.

9. When grief holds you back, move first. Grief and growth can coexist. You can honor what was lost while

building what comes next—carrying the grief with you as you go.

    10. When you've lost everything, move first. Sometimes we burn to the ground before we rise from the ashes. Your loss can be the clearing where something new grows.

    Because on the other side of "anyway" is the person you were always meant to become.

    The science is clear. Action creates feeling. Brains change. Cycles break. Transformation is possible.

    But knowing isn't doing.

    You have to move first. The feeling catches up.

YOUR MOVE FIRST TOOLKIT

Practical Exercises for Taking Action

Here are specific exercises you can use starting today.

Exercise 1: The Five-Minute Action

When you're stuck, overwhelmed, or paralyzed by the gap between where you are and where you want to be, use the five-minute action.

    Ask yourself: What is ONE thing I could do in the next five minutes that would move me in the right direction?

    Not the whole project. Not the complete transformation. Just five minutes.

    The action doesn't have to be big. It could be: - Writing one sentence - Sending one text - Taking one walk around the block - Doing one pushup - Reading one page - Making one phone call

    The point isn't the size of the action. The point is breaking the paralysis. Once you're in motion, it's easier to stay in motion. The five-minute action gets you moving.

    Exercise 2: The Implementation Intention

    Pick one change you want to make. Now make it specific using the if-then format:

"If \[situation\], then I will \[behavior\]."

Examples: - If it is 6 am, then I will put on my walking shoes and go outside. - If I feel the urge to drink, then I will call my support person. - If I finish my morning coffee, then I will write for 15 minutes. - If I feel overwhelmed, then I will take three deep breaths.

Write your implementation intention down. Put it somewhere you'll see it. The more specific your plan, the more likely you are to follow through.

Exercise 3: The Identity Question

Instead of asking "What do I want to achieve?" ask "Who do I want to become?"

Then ask: "What would that person do today?"

Write down three specific behaviors that align with your desired identity. These are your votes. Each time you do one of these behaviors, you're casting a vote for who you're becoming.

Exercise 4: The Opposite Action

Identify an emotion that's currently driving you in an unhelpful direction.

What is the emotion urging you to do?

Now, what is the opposite of that urge?

Fear urges avoidance → Approach Sadness urges withdrawal → Connect Shame urges hiding → Let yourself be seen Anger urges attack → Step back

Try the opposite action, gently and gradually. Notice how acting against the emotion's urge affects the emotion itself.

Exercise 5: The Stress Reframe

Next time you feel your stress response activate—heart pounding, palms sweating, stomach churning—try this reframe:

Instead of: "I'm so stressed. This is bad for me." Try: "My body is preparing me to meet this challenge. This response is helping me."

Notice that you're not denying the stress. You're reinterpreting it. Same physical sensations, different meaning.

Exercise 6: The Self-Compassion Break

When you're struggling or have made a mistake, try this three-part practice:

First, acknowledge the pain: "This is a moment of suffering. This is hard."

Second, remember common humanity: "Struggle is part of being human. I'm not alone in this."

Third, offer yourself kindness: "May I be kind to myself. May I give myself the compassion I need."

You can also ask: "What would I say to a good friend in this situation?" Then say that to yourself.

Exercise 7: The Tiny Habit

Identify a habit you want to build. Now make it tiny—so small you can't say no.

Want to meditate? Start with one breath. Want to exercise? Start with one pushup. Want to journal? Start with one sentence. Want to read? Start with one page.

Attach your tiny habit to something you already do: "After I [existing habit], I will [tiny new habit]."

Example: "After I pour my morning coffee, I will write one sentence in my journal."

Celebrate immediately after completing your tiny habit, even if it's just a mental "Nice job!" This positive emotion reinforces the behavior.

Exercise 8: The Evidence List

When your inner critic tells you that you're not capable, not worthy, not enough—fight back with evidence.

Make a list of times you've: - Survived something hard - Accomplished something you weren't sure you could - Helped someone else - Kept going when you wanted to quit - Learned something new - Recovered from a setback

These are your evidence. These prove your inner critic wrong. When the voice says "you can't," point to the list and say "I did."

Exercise 9: The Why Statement

Viktor Frankl taught that those with a why can bear any how. What's your why?

Complete this sentence: "I am working toward change because..."

Your why might be: - A person you love - A future you want to create - A past you refuse to repeat - A contribution you want to make - A version of yourself you want to become

Write your why somewhere visible. Return to it when the going gets hard.

Exercise 10: The Daily Check-In

Each day, take two minutes for this check-in:

Morning: "What is one thing I can do today that my future self will thank me for?"

Evening: "What is one thing I did today that I'm proud of, however small?"

This simple practice builds both intention and recognition—you start the day with purpose and end it with acknowledgment.

Putting It All Together

You don't need to use all these exercises at once. Pick one or two that resonate. Try them for a week. Notice what happens.

Remember: the exercises work because you do them, not because you read about them. Understanding is not doing. Knowledge is not action.

Move first. The feeling catches up. Start small. Be patient with yourself. And let the evidence accumulate.

RESOURCES FOR YOUR JOURNEY
Books That Have Helped Me:

"Man's Search for Meaning" by Viktor Frankl - The foundational text on finding meaning in suffering

"Daring Greatly" by Brené Brown - On vulnerability and shame resilience

"Atomic Habits" by James Clear - The practical guide to building habits that stick

"Grit" by Angela Duckworth - Why perseverance matters more than talent

"Mindset" by Carol Dweck - How your beliefs about yourself shape your potential

"The High 5 Habit" by Mel Robbins - Simple practice for building self-belief

"Tiny Habits" by BJ Fogg - The science of starting small

"The Upside of Stress" by Kelly McGonigal - Reframing your relationship with stress

"Self-Compassion" by Kristin Neff - Learning to treat yourself with kindness

"The Body Keeps the Score" by Bessel van der Kolk - Understanding trauma's impact on the body

"Rising Strong" by Brené Brown - The process of getting back up after falling

A Note on Professional Help:

This book is not a substitute for professional support. If you're struggling with trauma, addiction, depression, anxiety, or other mental health challenges, please reach out to a qualified professional.

There is no shame in getting help. In fact, seeking help is one of the bravest things you can do. It's the ultimate act of moving first—reaching out when everything in you wants to hide.

If you're in crisis: - National Suicide Prevention Lifeline: 988 - Crisis Text Line: Text HOME to 741741 - SAMHSA National Helpline: 1-800-662-4357

You are worth the help. You deserve support. And asking for it is strength, not weakness.

ADDITIONAL EXERCISES

Daily Practices and Deeper Work

Additional Reflection Exercises

The Power of Writing It Down

Research consistently shows that writing about our experiences—especially difficult ones—has measurable benefits for both mental and physical health. Dr. James Pennebaker at the University of Texas has conducted dozens of studies showing that expressive writing reduces stress, improves immune function, and helps people process trauma.

Here are some writing prompts to work through as you read this book:

The Letter You'll Never Send Write a letter to someone who hurt you, or to a younger version of yourself, or to someone you've lost. You don't have to send it—the power is in the writing itself. Say everything you've never been able to say.

The Story of Your Strength Write about a time when you showed strength you didn't know you had. What happened? What did you do? What did you learn about yourself?

The Person You're Becoming Write a letter from your future self—the version of you who has made it through, who has built the life you're working toward. What does that person want you to know? What encouragement do they have?

The Reframe Take something you've always seen as a failure or a flaw, and write about it from a different perspective. What did that experience teach you? How did it shape you in ways that might actually serve you?

Your Why Statement (Extended) Write at least a full page about why you want to change. Get specific. Get emotional. Don't censor yourself. This document is for you.

Daily Practices

Morning Intention (2 minutes) Before you start your day, ask: How do I want to show up today? What would my best self do?

The Pause Practice (30 seconds, multiple times daily) Several times throughout the day, pause. Just pause. Take three breaths. Notice how you're feeling. Notice what you're doing.

This simple practice builds the space between stimulus and response that Viktor Frankl wrote about. It interrupts autopilot. It reminds you that you have choice.

Evening Reflection (5 minutes) Reflect on: one thing you did well, one thing you learned, one thing you're grateful for.

Weekly Review (15 minutes) What went well? What was challenging? What do I want to focus on next week?

The Compassion Pause When you notice self-criticism arising—the harsh inner voice, the shame spiral—try this:

Stop. Place your hand on your heart. Say to yourself: "This is hard. I'm struggling. And that's okay." Ask: "What do I need right now?"

Sometimes what you need is rest. Sometimes it's connection. Sometimes it's action. But pausing to ask the question, with compassion, changes everything.

Working With Setbacks

Setbacks are information, not failures. When you experience one: get curious instead of critical, recommit immediately, reach out for support, and return to your why. A setback is a sign you're trying.

Building Your Support System

Identify your people—those who believe in you. Be specific about what you need. Create accountability. Limit exposure to saboteurs. Consider professional support. Find your community.

Building a life you're proud of is not a solo endeavor.

A FINAL WORD

What Comes Next

Reading this book will not change your life. I wish it could.

What changes your life is action. Repeated action. Daily action. Action even when you don't feel like it.

Move first. The feeling catches up.

The research is clear. The evidence is overwhelming. The path is known. But you have to walk it. No one can walk it for you.

I believe in you—not because I know you, but because I know what humans are capable of. I've seen it in the kids I've worked with, the ones everyone else had given up on. I've seen it in myself, the abandoned girl who became someone she never thought she could be. I've seen it in the research, study after study showing that change is possible at any age, from any starting point.

You are capable of more than you know. Your past does not determine your future. Your current feelings are not accurate predictors of what you can accomplish.

Start small. Start today. Start imperfect.

And when you don't feel ready—when fear says stay small, when doubt says why bother, when your history says you can't—move first. The feeling catches up.

Because on the other side of anyway is the person you were always meant to become.

And I can't wait to meet them.

With love and belief in your capacity to change, Sam

ACKNOWLEDGMENTS

To Thomas: You saved my life before you even knew you could. Being your mother has been the greatest privilege of my existence. Watching you grow into the man you're becoming—thoughtful, wise, breaking cycles I couldn't break—fills me with a pride I don't have words for. Thank you for choosing good. Thank you for being you. I love you more than this book could ever express.

To Jose: Seventeen years. Seventeen years of you showing up, even when I pushed you away. Seventeen years of patience I didn't deserve and love I didn't know how to receive. You saw me at my worst and stayed anyway. You fell in love with my son before you fell in love with me, and that's how I knew you were different. Thank you for being my partner on this messy, imperfect, beautiful journey. I love you.

To my father: Our relationship was complicated. You were imperfect. You struggled with demons you never conquered. But you came for me when I needed rescuing. You loved me the best way you knew how. I wish you'd found healing before you died. I hope, wherever you are, you've finally found peace. Rest now, Dad.

To my sister, Ali: I'm sorry I haven't always been the most present. I've been working through things quietly, finding my way in my own time. Please know that I am always here for you, and I love you more than you know. We are the last of Dad, and that truth binds us in a way that is deep, enduring, and uniquely ours. We will always share a bond that nothing can take away.

To my grandma: you are the most incredible, caring soul I have ever known. You see me at my core, understand me without needing words, and protect me in the moments I need it most. Your love has been a constant source of safety, strength, and belonging in my life. You have always been my role model, the standard I look up to, and the kind of woman I hope to embody. I admire you more than you will ever understand, and I carry your influence with me in everything I do.

To Mel Robbins: You'll probably never read this, but I need to thank you anyway. Your work changed my life. Your voice in my headphones kept me company on walks and workouts and mornings when I needed someone to tell me I could do hard things. "Move first" became my mantra because of you. Thank you for being so generously, authentically yourself.

To Bruno, Otis, and Lyla: My babies. My companions. The creatures who get me out of bed when depression tries to keep me there. You don't care about my trauma or my achievements or my failures. You just want walks and treats and belly rubs. Thank you for the simple joy of your presence.

To the children I've worked with over fifteen years: You taught me more than any training ever could. You showed me what resilience looks like in its rawest form. You reminded me why this work matters. I carry you with me, all of you, in everything I do.

And to you, the reader: Thank you for trusting me with your time and your attention. Thank you for being brave enough to pick up this book. I don't know your story, but I know you have one. And I know it matters. Keep going. Keep healing. Keep believing you're worthy.

Because you are.

ABOUT THE AUTHOR

Samantha Teeboon never expected to write a book. Growing up, she was too busy surviving to imagine a future that included sharing her story with the world.

Born into chaos and raised in instability, Sam learned early that life wasn't going to hand her anything. She was abandoned at four years old, spending nights alone in dark houses while her mother was on the streets. She lost her friend in a car accident at age six. She became pregnant at fifteen and escaped an abusive relationship at seventeen.

By any reasonable measure, the odds were stacked against her.

But Sam refused to let her past determine her future. Even when she was drowning—in trauma, in addiction, in the belief that she was fundamentally broken—something in her kept fighting. Something kept showing up. Something kept taking the next small step, even when she couldn't see where the path was leading.

That something is what she now calls "move first. The feeling catches up."

Today, Sam has over fifteen years of experience working with children who have experienced trauma. She has worked with some of the most challenging students in the school system—the kids everyone else has given up on—and she sees herself in every single one of them. She knows what it's like to be written off, and she knows what it's like to prove people wrong.

Sam holds a bachelor's degree in Psychology—a degree that took her ten years to complete, earned while working full-time and raising her son. She graduated in 2025 at age thirty-five, living proof that it's never too late and there's no "right" timeline for achievement. She is currently pursuing her master's degree.

She is the founder of Compass Behavior Support, a virtual parent coaching business where she helps families navigate behavioral challenges using evidence-based strategies and a whole lot of compassion. She believes that every parent is doing the best they can with what they have, and that with the right support, families can transform.

Sam lives in Rochester, New York, with her husband Jose—who has stood by her side for seventeen years, even when she tried to push him away—and their son Thomas, now nineteen. Thomas, she'll tell you, is her greatest achievement. Watching him grow into a thoughtful, wise young man who is breaking generational cycles fills her with a pride she doesn't have adequate words to express.

She also shares her home with three pit bulls—Bruno, Otis, and Lyla—who keep her grounded, get her outside every day, and remind her that sometimes the most healing thing in the world is a walk in the morning sun with beings who love you unconditionally.

When she's not working, studying, or caring for her family, Sam can be found drinking coffee and watching the sunrise, taking her dogs on adventures, and planning for the RV life she and Jose hope to build in the coming years—a life of freedom and adventure that the abandoned little girl in the dark house never could have imagined.

"Move First" is her first book. She wrote it because she needed it—and because she believes someone else needs it too. If her story can help even one person find the courage to take action before they feel ready, then every word was worth writing.

Connect with Sam:

Website: samanthateeboon.com

Email: sam@samanthateeboon.com

If this book has helped you, Sam would love to hear from you. And if you're in the middle of your own struggle, she wants you to know: you're not alone, it's possible, and you can do this.

Move first. The feeling catches up.

You picked up this book for a reason.

Don't just read about moving first — do it.

Scan this code and grab your free guide: *5 Questions to Ask Before You Leap*

This is your first move.

www.ingramcontent.com/pod-product-compliance
Lightning Source LLC
Chambersburg PA
CBHW060428130626
46555CB00005B/2262